ACCOUNTING and AUDITING RESEARCH:
A Practical Guide

Thomas R. Weirich, PhD, CPA
Professor of Accounting
Central Michigan University

David J. Karmon, MS, CPA
Assistant Professor of Accounting
Central Michigan University

9892772

Published by

A91 **SOUTH-WESTERN PUBLISHING CO.**

CINCINNATI   WEST CHICAGO, ILL.   DALLAS   PELHAM MANOR, N.Y.   PALO ALTO, CALIF.

ISBN: 0–538–01910–7

Library of Congress Catalog Card Number: 83–60657

2345K76543

Printed in the United States of America

PREFACE

A concern exists among educators and practitioners alike as to the ability of accountants to effectively research practical accounting and auditing issues. It is apparent that with the increasing complexity of the accounting and auditing environment and the continuously changing professional standards, the practitioner should be able to resolve complex accounting or auditing questions on a timely basis. Therefore, this text features a practical methodology for conducting efficient and effective accounting and auditing research.

In a sense, this text is a do-it-yourself, understand-it-yourself manual which serves as a primer on methodology to assist the practitioner in conducting accounting and auditing research. The text is a practical manual which guides the reader, step by step, through the research process. Every attempt is made to communicate with clarity to the reader a basic framework which should assist in the research process of defining the accounting or auditing issue, conducting the research, documenting and evaluating the research findings, and drawing conclusions.

The text is structured to first present an overview of the research process in the accounting and auditing environment followed by applications of the methodology to specific case illustrations. Chapter 1 presents an introduction to accounting and auditing research. Chapters 2 and 3 focus on an overview of the environment of accounting and auditing research with an emphasis on the standard-setting process. The meaning of the term "generally accepted accounting principles" is discussed as well as the role that professional judgment plays in the research process. Chapter 4 begins a detailed analysis of the research process with Chapters 5 and 6 presenting a discussion of the many sources of authoritative literature and various access techniques to the professional literature. Chapter 7 concludes with a refinement of the research process. This text will familiarize the reader with the many available research tools with special emphasis on the use of the American Institute of Certified Public Accountants' *Index to Accounting and Auditing Technical Pronouncements* and *Professional Standards* series as well as the Financial Accounting Standards Board's *Accounting Standards* series. Moreover, the text provides a number of cases which should give the reader practical experience in utilizing these research tools.

At the collegiate level, this text should serve well as a supplement to intermediate and advanced accounting and auditing classes. The text will provide the student with the "what," "why," and "how" of conducting practical accounting and auditing research. Also presented in the text are comprehensive listings of sources of authoritative and semiauthoritative support to aid in researching complex accounting and auditing problems. Utilized by the practitioner, this text will serve as a reference in providing a framework for resolving the day-to-day accounting or auditing issues confronted. The text could be used in staff training courses as an aid in teaching practical accounting or auditing research.

We greatly appreciate the permission from the AICPA to include liberal quotations from official pronouncements and page illustrations of various publications. Also appreciated are the reviews and suggestions offered by David Simmons, Touche Ross & Co., Detroit, and James Aitken, formerly with Ernst & Whinney, Lansing. However, all limitations of the text are the sole responsibility of the authors.

Thomas R. Weirich
David J. Karmon

CONTENTS

Chapter 1

INTRODUCTION TO
ACCOUNTING
AND AUDITING RESEARCH

Hardly a day goes by in which the professional accountant, whether in public accounting, industry, or government, does not become involved in the investigation and analysis of an accounting or auditing issue. The issue or problem must be clearly defined, facts gathered, authoritative literature reviewed, alternatives evaluated, and conclusions drawn. In conducting this research process, the researcher must answer three basic questions:

1. Does authoritative literature exist as to the issue under review?
2. If authoritative literature does exist, how does the researcher develop a conclusion in an efficient and effective way?
3. If authoritative literature does not exist, what approach does the researcher follow in arriving at a conclusion?

The purpose of this text is to provide the understanding and the research skills needed to answer these questions. The "what," "why," and "how" of practical accounting and auditing research are discussed with emphasis on the following topics: What are generally accepted accounting principles and generally accepted auditing standards? What constitutes substantial authoritative support? What are the available sources of current accounting and auditing literature? A practical research approach is presented, along with discussions of various research tools. This research approach is demonstrated through the use of a number of practice problems presented as case studies.

Nature of Accounting and Auditing Research

This text focuses on accounting and auditing research within the practicing segment of the accounting profession in contrast to theoretical research often conducted by academicians. Today's practitioner must be able to properly conduct research in a systematic fashion to arrive at appropriate and timely conclusions regarding the issues at hand. Efficient and effective accounting or auditing research is often necessary in order to determine the proper recording, classification, and disclosure of economic events; to determine compliance with authoritative accounting or auditing pronouncements; or to determine the preferability of alternative accounting procedures.

Examples of issues frequently encountered by the practitioner include such questions as: What are the accounting or auditing implications of a new transaction? Is the accounting treatment of the transaction in agreement with generally accepted accounting principles? What are the financial statement disclosure requirements? What is the auditor's association and responsibility when confronted with supplemental information presented in annual reports but not as part of the basic financial statements?

Finding answers to these often-complex questions is becoming more difficult and time-consuming as the financial accounting and reporting requirements and the auditing standards increase in number and complexity. The research process is often further complicated when the accountant or auditor is researching a practical issue for which no authoritative literature exists, or the authoritative literature does not directly address the question.

Role of Research in the Public Accounting Firm

Although research is often conducted by accountants in industry or government, accounting and auditing research is particularly important in the public accounting firm. Due to the number and diversity of clients served, public accounting firms are constantly engaged in conducting research on a wide range of accounting and auditing issues.

Many of the larger multioffice firms maintain their own research departments. A typical organizational structure for policy decision making and research on accounting and auditing matters within a firm is depicted in Figure 1-1.

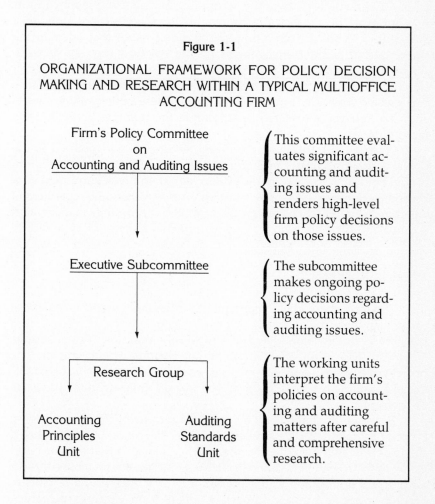

Figure 1-1

ORGANIZATIONAL FRAMEWORK FOR POLICY DECISION MAKING AND RESEARCH WITHIN A TYPICAL MULTIOFFICE ACCOUNTING FIRM

Firm's Policy Committee on Accounting and Auditing Issues

This committee evaluates significant accounting and auditing issues and renders high-level firm policy decisions on those issues.

Executive Subcommittee

The subcommittee makes ongoing policy decisions regarding accounting and auditing issues.

Research Group

The working units interpret the firm's policies on accounting and auditing matters after careful and comprehensive research.

Accounting Principles Unit

Auditing Standards Unit

The responsibilities of a firm-wide accounting and auditing policy decision function include: maintaining a high level of professional competence in accounting and auditing matters; developing and rendering high-level policies and procedures on accounting and auditing issues for the firm; disseminating the firm's policies and procedures to appropriate personnel within the firm on a timely basis; and supervising the quality control of the firm's practice. Research plays an important role in the decision-making process.

The Policy Committee and Executive Subcommittee, as shown in Figure 1-1, generally consist of highly competent audit partners with years of practical experience. The Policy Committee's primary function is to evaluate significant accounting and auditing issues and establish firm-wide policies on these issues. The Executive Subcommittee handles the daily ongoing policy decisions (lower-level decisions) for the firm as a whole. The responsibility of the accounting and auditing research units is to interpret firm policies in the context of specific client situations. Frequently, technical accounting and auditing issues that arise during the course of a client engagement can be resolved through research conducted by personnel assigned to the engagement. When a matter cannot be satisfactorily resolved at the local-office level, assistance is requested from the firm's research units. These units conduct careful and comprehensive research in arriving at the firm's response to technical inquiries.

Practical accounting and auditing research is not confined to the public accounting firm. Every practitioner should possess the ability to conduct efficient research and develop logical and well-supported conclusions on a timely basis. The research process is the same regardless of whether the researcher is engaged in public accounting, management accounting, internal auditing, or governmental accounting or auditing.

What Is Research?

The term "research" has frequently been misunderstood by those unfamiliar with the research process, which is often perceived as a mechanical process conducted in a mystical environment by a strange individual. The approach is anything but mystical or mechanistic. The process of conducting any type of research, including practical accounting and auditing research, is simply a systematic investigation of an issue or problem.

Research in general can be classified into two primary categories: (1) pure research and (2) applied research. *Pure research,* often labeled *basic research,* involves the investigation of questions that appear interesting to the researcher, generally an academician, but may have little or no practical application at the present time. For example, a researcher may be interested in the impact of inflation on earnings per share figures and security prices.[1] Such research has little present practical application and can be referred to as *empirical research,* i.e., research based upon experiment or observation. However, pure or basic research should not be discounted as worthless. Such research adds to

---

[1] William A. Hillison, "Empirical Investigation of General Purchasing Power Adjustments on Earnings per Share and the Movement of Security Prices," *Journal of Accounting Research* (Spring, 1979), pp. 60-73.

the body of knowledge in a particular field and may ultimately contribute directly or indirectly to practical problem solutions. Empirical research studies, for example, are frequently reviewed and evaluated by standard-setting bodies in drafting authoritative accounting and auditing pronouncements.

Applied research, which is the focus of this text, involves the investigation of an issue of immediate practical importance. For example, assume that a public accounting firm has been asked to evaluate a client's proposed new accounting treatment for self-insurance. The client expects an answer within two days as to the acceptability of the new method and the impact it would have on the financial statements. In such a case, a member of the accounting firm's professional staff would investigate authoritative literature as to the acceptability of the method or develop a logical theoretical justification for or against the new method if no authoritative literature exists on the topic.

The applied research in the preceding example can be subcategorized as *a priori* (before the fact) research. In other words, the research is conducted before the client actually enters into a transaction. On the other hand, a client may request advice relating to a transaction that has already been executed. Research relating to a completed transaction or other past event is referred to as *a posteriori* (after the fact) research. There are frequently advantages to conducting *a priori* as opposed to *a posteriori* research. For example, if research reveals that a proposed transaction will have an unfavorable impact on financial statements, the transaction can be abandoned or possibly restructured to avoid undesirable consequences. These options are not available, however, once a transaction is completed.

There is a need to conduct both pure and applied research. If either type of research is conducted properly, the methodology is the same, only the environment differs. Both types of research require sound research design to effectively and efficiently resolve the issue under investigation.

Overview of the Research Process

The research process in general is often defined as the *scientific method of inquiry*, a systematic study of a particular field of knowledge in order to discover scientific facts or principles. The basic purpose of research, therefore, is to obtain knowledge or information that specifically pertains to some issue or problem. An operational definition of research encompasses the following elements:[2]

---

[2]David J. Luck, Hugh C. Wales, and Donald A. Taylor, *Marketing Research* (Englewood Cliffs: Prentice-Hall, Inc., 1961), p. 5.

1. There must be an orderly investigation and analysis of a clearly defined issue or problem.
2. An appropriate scientific approach must be used.
3. Adequate and representative evidence must be gathered and documented.
4. Logical reasoning must be employed in drawing conclusions.
5. The researcher must be able to support the validity or reasonableness of the conclusions.

With this general understanding of the research process, practical accounting and auditing research may be defined as follows:

Accounting or auditing research — A systematic and logical approach to obtaining and documenting evidence underlying a conclusion relating to an accounting or auditing issue or problem currently confronting the accountant or auditor.

The basic steps in the research process are illustrated in Figure 1-2 and discussed in the following sections. As indicated in the illustration, each step of the research process should be carefully documented.

Identify the Issue. In many cases, the basic issue has already been identified before the research process begins, e.g., when a client requests advice as to the proper handling of a specific transaction. However, further identification of the exact issue is often required. This process of refining the issue at hand is referred to as *problem distillation,* whereby a general issue is restated in sufficiently specific terms. If the statement of the issue is too broad or general, the researcher is apt to waste valuable time consulting sources which are not relevant to the specific issue.

Factors to consider in the identification and statement of the issue include the exact source of the issue, justification for the issue, and a determination of the scope of the issue. To successfully design and execute an investigation, the issue must be clearly stated.

Collect Evidence. Once the issue is adequately defined, the researcher is ready to proceed with step two of the research process, the collection of evidence. The research begins with the development of a plan that carefully presents the procedures to follow in collecting evidence. The actual collection of evidence will usually encompass a detailed review of relevant authoritative accounting or auditing literature and a survey of present practice. A number of research tools that will aid in the collection of evidence are available and are discussed in detail in Chapters 4 through 6. In cases where authoritative literature does not exist on a specific issue, the accountant or auditor needs to develop a theoretical resolution of the issue based upon a logical analysis of the factors involved.

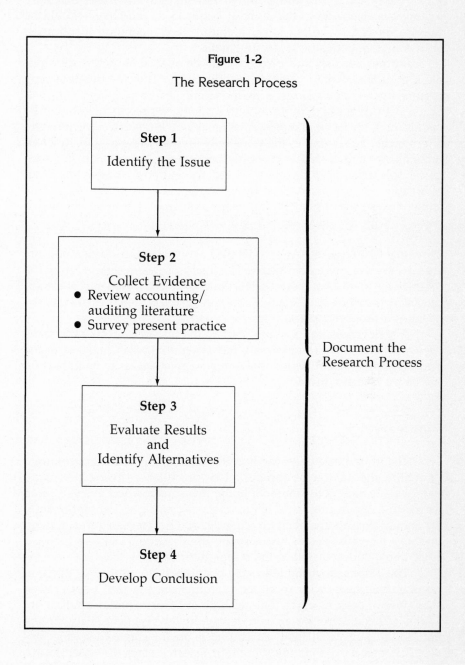

Figure 1-2

The Research Process

Step 1

Identify the Issue

Step 2

Collect Evidence
- Review accounting/ auditing literature
- Survey present practice

Step 3

Evaluate Results
and
Identify Alternatives

Step 4

Develop Conclusion

Document the
Research Process

Evaluate Results and Identify Alternatives. Once a thorough investigation and collection of evidence has been completed, the next step is to evaluate the results and identify alternatives to arrive at one or more tentative conclusions to the issue at hand. Each alternative should be fully supported by authoritative literature or a theoretical justification with complete and concise documentation.

Further analysis and research may be needed as to the appropriateness of the various alternatives identified. This reevaluation may require further discussions with the client or consultations with colleagues. In discussing an issue with a client, the researcher should be cognizant of the fact that management may not be objective in evaluating alternatives. For example, the issue may involve the acceptability of an accounting method that is currently being used by the client. In such cases, the research is directed toward the support or rejection of an alternative already decided on by management. The possibility of bias should cause the researcher to retain a degree of skepticism in discussions with the client regarding a conclusion.

Develop Conclusion. After a detailed analysis of the alternatives, the researcher develops a conclusion. The final conclusion selected from the alternatives identified should be thoroughly documented and well supported by the evidence gathered. The conclusion is then presented to the client as a proposed solution to the issue.

A serious weakness in any part of the research process threatens the worth of the entire research effort. Therefore, each segment of the process should be addressed with equal seriousness as to its impact on the entire research project.

Summary

The importance of research in the work of a practicing accountant or auditor should now be apparent. Few practitioners ever experience a workweek which does not include the investigation and analysis of an accounting or auditing issue. Thus, every practicing accountant or auditor should possess the ability to conduct practical research in a systematic way. The goal of this text is to aid the practitioner in developing a basic framework to assist in the research process.

The emphasis of the following chapters is on applied or practical research that deals with solutions to immediate practical issues rather than pure or basic research that has little or no present day application. Chapters 2 and 3 provide an overview of the environment of accounting and auditing research, with an emphasis on the standard-setting process. Chapter 4 expands upon the four research steps discussed in this chapter and applies the steps to an illustrative problem. Chapter 5 presents a discussion of the sources of authoritative literature as well as an explanation of access techniques to the professional literature. Chapter 6 discusses other available research tools that may aid in the efficient and effective conduct of practical research. Chapter 7 concludes with a refinement of the research process by presenting specific annotated steps and formatting procedures for conducting and documenting the research process via a comprehensive problem.

DISCUSSION QUESTIONS

1. Why is accounting or auditing research necessary?
2. What is the objective of accounting or auditing research?
3. Describe the role of research within the public accounting firm.
4. Differentiate between pure and applied research.
5. Distinguish between *a priori* and *a posteriori* research.
6. Explain the four steps involved in the accounting or auditing research process.
7. Discuss how research can support or refute a biased alternative.
8. Explain what is meant by problem distillation and its importance in the research process.

Chapter 2

THE ENVIRONMENT OF
ACCOUNTING RESEARCH

In researching an accounting issue, the practitioner must be cognizant of the professional and business environment. The practitioner does not operate in a stagnant environment, but one that is very dynamic. New professional standards are constantly being issued, and existing standards are being updated or completely deleted. The following list includes major environmental factors that influence the development of accounting standards:

1. Requirements of governmental and other regulatory bodies.
2. Influence of various tax laws on the financial reporting process.
3. Practices or problems of certain specialized industries, such as the motion picture and oil and gas industries.
4. Inconsistencies in practice.
5. Disagreement among accountants, business executives, and others as to the objectives of financial statements.
6. Various professional organizations.

In such an environment, the practitioner needs to be aware of the changes taking place and environmental influences in order to properly analyze a research problem. The objective of this chapter is to present an overview of the environment of accounting research with a discussion of the accounting standard-setting process. Emphasis will be directed toward two questions: (1) What constitutes generally accepted accounting principles (GAAP)? and (2) What is the hierarchy of authoritative support? The subsequent chapter will focus on the environment of auditing research and the role of professional judgment in the research process.

Standard-Setting Environment

The necessity for the establishment of accounting standards has evolved over time in order to meet the needs of users of financial statements. A review of the past sixty to seventy years reveals a vast increase in the number of financial statement users (primarily investors, lenders, and governmental entities), as well as an increase in the complexity of business enterprise. These evolutionary changes have resulted in a greater demand by financial statement users for increased uniformity in accounting principles and procedures to aid comparability of financial statements among entities. Many of the standards issued by authoritative accounting bodies have attempted to address this issue of comparability through the reduction of the inconsistencies in accounting practice. Although financial statement users have generally been the primary concern in the development of accounting principles or standards, many professional organizations, governmental agencies, and legislative acts have a significant impact on the final standards issued.

Accounting Standard-Setting Process

Accounting standard-setting in the private sector is currently the responsibility of the Financial Accounting Standards Board (FASB). Prior to formation of the FASB, the American Institute of Certified Public Accountants (AICPA) was the recognized standard-setting body. In the public sector, accounting standards applicable to certain companies are established by various governmental entities, including the Securities and Exchange Commission (SEC), the Cost Accounting Standards Board (CASB), and the National Council on Governmental Accounting (NCGA). A number of professional organizations and public accounting firms are also involved in the standard-setting process. Although these groups do not establish standards, they provide input into the development of the standards.

The following sections present an overview of the organizations that impact the standard-setting process. Also discussed briefly are the major pronouncements issued by each authoritative body.

American Institute of Certified Public Accountants. The AICPA is the national professional organization for certified public accountants and was the designated standard-setting body prior to formation of the FASB in 1973. Authoritative pronouncements were issued by two designated bodies within the AICPA:

1. Committee on Accounting Procedures (1939-1959)
2. Accounting Principles Board (1959-1973)

In 1938 the AICPA established the Committee on Accounting Procedures (CAP) to issue pronouncements on generally accepted accounting principles. This committee issued a series of pronouncements entitled *Accounting Research Bulletins*. Of the first 42 bulletins issued, eight represented reports of the AICPA's Committee on Terminology. In 1953 these were consolidated and published as *Accounting Terminology Bulletin No. 1*. The remaining research bulletins, which addressed specific accounting principles and procedures, were consolidated and published as *Accounting Research Bulletin No. 43*. Between 1953 and 1959, eight more research bulletins and three additional terminology bulletins were issued.

During 1959 the Accounting Principles Board replaced the Committee on Accounting Procedures as the committee of the AICPA responsible for establishing accounting standards. The APB remained in existence from 1959 to 1973 and issued 31 authoritative pronouncements entitled *Opinions of the Accounting Principles Board*. The APB also issued four Statements, which addressed broad concepts rather than specific accounting principles, and a number of unofficial Interpretations.

Although the FASB has replaced the AICPA as the accounting standard-setting body, the Accounting Research Bulletins and APB Opinions which have not been superseded or modified remain in effect. Also, the AICPA continues to exert significant influence on the standard-setting process. Various committees of the AICPA publish *Industry Accounting Guides*, and the Accounting Standards Division of the Institute publishes *Statements of Position* (SOPs). These publications represent the Institute's position on the application of accounting principles to particular industries or special areas.

Financial Accounting Standards Board. The FASB, established in 1973, is the current accounting standard-setting body. Unlike its predecessors, the CAP and APB, the FASB is not a committee of the AICPA, but an independent seven-member board. The FASB's authoritative pronouncements on accounting principles or standards are labeled *Statements of Financial Accounting Standards*. The FASB also issued *Interpretations of Financial Accounting Standards*, which interpret Accounting Research Bulletins and APB Opinions, as well as FASB Statements of Financial Accounting Standards.

The staff of the FASB has been authorized to issue *Technical Bulletins,* which are unofficial interpretations designed to give timely advice on the application of accounting standards.

Procedures for Establishing FASB Standards. The rule-making or due-process procedures of the FASB for the establishment of accounting standards is structured as follows:

1. *Problem identification.* Accounting issues and problems are brought to the FASB's attention from many different sources, such as the SEC, public accounting firms, industry associations, academicians, and others. The issues raised may be very conceptual in nature or very specific.
2. *Establishment of task force.* After consultation with its technical staff, the FASB determines whether an issue will be placed on its agenda. If necessary, a task force is established to aid in the definition of the problem and to conduct research.
3. *Issuance of a discussion memorandum.* For major projects, the Board issues a neutral-view discussion memorandum which presents the issue and alternative solutions and requests comments from interested parties.
4. *Public hearing.* Although not mandatory, a public hearing is usually held on major projects to provide an opportunity for anyone to speak on an issue. In addition to the input provided through these hearings, a number of comment letters are received by the Board from interested parties concerning points raised in the discussion memorandum. After analyzing the responses to a discussion memorandum, the Board may choose to issue an exposure draft, which represents a proposed or tentative statement.
5. *Issuance of exposure draft.* An exposure draft, as well as a final standard, contains a statement of the standard, background information, the basis for the Board's conclusions, and an effective date for the standard. The exposure period for public comment is normally at least 60 days. After further deliberation and evaluation of comments received, the Board may issue a final statement.
6. *Issuance of FASB statement.* The standard-setting process concludes with a vote on the proposed statement. If a majority of the seven Board members vote in favor of a proposed statement, a final statement is issued.

FASB's Conceptual Framework Project. In certain situations, an accounting issue may arise for which no precedent has been set and no authoritative pronouncement has been issued. In such cases, the researcher must develop a theoretically justifiable conclusion. A number of organizations and individuals have directed their efforts toward the development of accounting theory in order to provide a framework for resolving issues in a theoretically consistent manner.

The American Accounting Association, a national professional organization with a membership composed primarily of academicians, sponsors and conducts extensive research of a theoretical or conceptual nature. The AICPA also promotes research in accounting theory and has published a series of *Accounting Research Monographs*. As mentioned previously, the Accounting Principles Board of the AICPA issued four conceptual statements during its existence.

Despite these and other efforts, however, a widely accepted theoretical framework of accounting has not been developed. Recognizing the need for such a framework, the FASB has undertaken a comprehensive, long-range project called the Conceptual Framework Project. This project encompasses a series of pronouncements entitled *Statements of Financial Accounting Concepts*, which describe concepts and relationships that underlie financial accounting standards. These pronouncements have addressed or will address such issues as the following: elements of financial statements and their recognition, measurement, and display; capital maintenance; unit of measure; criteria for distinguishing information to be included in financial statements from that which should be provided by other means of financial reporting; and criteria for evaluating and selecting accounting information (qualitative characteristics).

Statements of Financial Accounting Concepts Nos. 1-4, the first four statements issued under the Conceptual Framework Project, are as follows:

1. "Objectives of Financial Reporting of Business Enterprises." This statement sets forth the objectives of general purpose external financial reporting by business enterprises.
2. "Qualitative Characteristics of Accounting Information." This statement examines the characteristics of accounting information that make the information useful.
3. "Elements of Financial Statements of Business Enterprises." This statement defines 10 elements of financial statements of business enterprises: assets, liabilities, equity, investment by owners, distributions to owners, comprehensive income, revenues, expenses, gains, and losses.
4. "Objectives of Financial Reporting by Nonbusiness Organizations." This statement establishes the objectives of general purpose external financial reporting by nonbusiness organizations.

The FASB's Conceptual Framework Project and related pronouncements may serve as the foundation for resolving accounting issues not addressed by an authoritative body.

Securities and Exchange Commission. The SEC receives its authoritative status from the public sector rather than the accounting profession. The Securities and Exchange Act of 1934 established the SEC and charged it with the duty of insuring full and fair disclosures of all material facts relating to publicly traded securities. Power was given to the SEC to specify the form of documents filed with the Commission and to prescribe the accounting principles used in generating the financial data presented in the reports.

The Commission publishes four basic documents delineating its reporting and disclosure requirements:

1. *Regulation S-X* — describes the types of reports that must be filed and the forms that are to be used.
2. *Regulation S-K, Integrated Disclosure Rules* — prescribes the filing requirements for information presented outside the financial statements required under Regulation S-X.
3. *Financial Reporting Releases (FRRs)* — prescribe the accounting principles that must be followed in preparing reports filed with the Commission. These FRRs are analogous to the authoritative pronouncements of the APB or FASB.
4. *Accounting and Auditing Enforcement Releases (AAERs)* — relate to enforcement of the Commission's reporting and disclosure requirements.

The FRRs and AAERs were first issued in 1982. These new series of pronouncements replaced the SEC's *Accounting Series Releases (ASRs)*, which were issued from 1937 to 1982. Nonenforcement-related ASRs which are still in effect have been codified by the SEC. The Commission has published a topical index to enforcement-related ASRs.

The SEC also publishes a series of *Staff Accounting Bulletins*, which are unofficial interpretations of the SEC's prescribed accounting principles. These bulletins are analogous to the FASB Technical Bulletins.

The SEC has delegated the major responsibility for accounting standard-setting to the FASB but has retained an oversight function. This in essence is the recognition by the SEC of the authoritative support of accounting principles promulgated by the FASB. The Commission recognizes these principles as acceptable for use in filings with the Commission.

Cost Accounting Standards Board. The CASB was established by an act of Congress in 1970. From 1971 to 1980 the Board had the authority to promulgate cost accounting standards designed to achieve uniformity and consistency in the cost accounting principles followed by defense contractors and subcontractors. Subsequently, the standards of the CASB were extended to most nondefense contracts. The standards are thus applied to substantially all Federal Government contracts. The CASB operated until 1980 when Congress decided not to authorize funds for the Board's continuance. During its nine-year life, the Board published a number of CASB Standards and Interpretations which still remain in force.

National Council on Governmental Accounting. The NCGA, the standard-setting body of the Municipal Finance Officers' Association, is recognized by the AICPA as an authoritative rule-making body for governmental entities. In 1968, the National Committee on Governmental Accounting, predecessor to the NCGA, published *Governmental Accounting, Auditing and Financial Reporting* (GAAFR). In 1974, the AICPA industry audit guide, *Audits of State and Local Governmental Units*, recognized GAAFR as being an authoritative source in the area of accounting for state and local governmental units.[1]

In March 1979, the NCGA issued *Statement No. 1*, "Governmental Accounting and Financial Principles." This statement specified the basic general purpose financial statements of governmental units, and it updated and clarified portions of GAAFR. The AICPA *Statement of Position 80-2*, "Accounting and Financial Reporting by Governmental Units," states that financial statements prepared in accordance with Statement No. 1 are in conformity with generally accepted accounting principles.[2]

Discussion is presently taking place for the development of a Governmental Accounting Standards Board (GASB). A Governmental Accounting Standards Board Organization Committee composed of representatives from various organizations has recommended that the GASB serve as a parallel entity to the FASB. The purpose of the GASB would be to set financial accounting standards for state and local governmental entities.

Professional Organizations. The National Association of Accountants (NAA), through its Management Accounting Practices (MAP) Committee, provides formal input to the FASB in the standard-setting process. Although the NAA does not issue any authoritative pronouncements, the organization has been influential in the process of establishing accounting standards.

The Financial Executives Institute (FEI) influences accounting standards development through its Panel on Accounting Principles. This panel reviews, evaluates, and makes recommendations as to the various Discussion Memorandums issued by the FASB. The FEI also conducts its own research through the Financial Executives Research Foundation.

Generally Accepted Accounting Principles

Management has the responsibility for presenting financial statements that reflect the economic events and transactions in conformity with generally accepted accounting principles. The auditor's role is to

---

[1]*AICPA Technical Practice Aids*, Volume 2 (Chicago: Commerce Clearing House), Sec. 10,310.01.

[2]*Ibid.*, Sec. 10,310.02.

evaluate the appropriateness of management's selection and the application of the accounting principles employed. Thus, the accounting practitioner's research efforts (management accountant or auditor) are directed to the discovery or the evaluation of accounting principles and procedures that are considered generally accepted. The initial question then to ask is, What constitutes generally accepted accounting principles? There is no simple answer to this question. A subcommittee of the Accounting Principles Board worked on the project entitled "Basic Concepts and Broad Accounting Principles" in which they give some direction to defining GAAP:

> Generally accepted accounting principles are primarily conventional in nature. They are the result of decisions; they represent the consensus at any time as to how the financial accounting process should operate and how financial statements should be prepared from the information made available through the financial accounting process.
>
> Inasmuch as generally accepted accounting principles embody a consensus, they depend heavily on notions such as "general acceptance" and "substantial authoritative support," which have not been and probably will not be precisely defined. There is concurrence, however, that the notions of "general acceptance" and "substantial authoritative support" relate to the propriety of the practice, as viewed by informed intelligent and experienced accountants in the light of the purposes and limitations of the financial accounting process.[3]

More specifically, the APB has defined generally accepted accounting principles as "the conventions, rules, and procedures necessary to define accepted accounting practice at a particular time."[4] Thus, GAAP is not limited to the principles and procedures in pronouncements issued by authoritative bodies, but also includes practices that have achieved general acceptance over time.

The researcher should be aware of some basic characteristics of GAAP. First, GAAP is not a static well-defined set of accounting principles, but rather a fluid set of principles dependent upon contemporary accounting thought. As the business environment changes, certain principles may be discarded from use, while new principles may evolve to accommodate new business transactions. The researcher must be aware of these changes in the business environment to determine whether a particular principle or procedure is currently accepted, has been discarded as no longer appropriate, or is gaining support as an evolving new principle. This changing environment is evidenced by the fact that

---

[3]Marshall Armstrong, "Some Thoughts on Substantial Authoritative Support," *Journal of Accountancy* (April 1969), p. 50.

[4]*Accounting Principles Board Statement No. 4*, "Basic Concepts and Accounting Principles Underlying Financial Statements of Business Enterprises" (New York: American Institute of Certified Public Accountants, 1970), par. 138.

many FASB Statements have superseded or amended prior FASB Statements and pronouncements of the APB and CAP. Thus, the researcher must take steps to determine that a particular pronouncement has not been superseded or amended before relying on the pronouncement as a basis for developing conclusions.

Secondly, GAAP is not composed of mutually exclusive accounting principles. Alternative principles for similar transactions may be considered equally acceptable. The researcher must not end the search when one acceptable principle is found. He or she should continue to look for alternatives and must determine the weight of support for each alternative. Also, there are frequently alternative methods for applying a specific accounting principle, such as various rates for imputed interest in APB Opinion No. 21. Selecting from among the many alternatives requires the exercise of professional judgment as discussed in Chapter 3.

Finally, there has been and continues to be a strong emphasis on financial statement disclosure. Disclosure is a direct result of alternative choices and the need to qualify the numbers presented in the financial statements. Thus, the researcher must also be aware of the disclosure requirements for particular accounting principles.

Authoritative Support

Accounting is not a natural science nor even a social science. Research conducted in the area of the sciences is an attempt to develop a theory or model that describes observed phenomena and makes predictions of future events. Accounting is not a theory in this scientific sense. Rather, accounting is a systematic process designed to accumulate economic data and report these data to users of such information. The accounting practitioner does not search for natural laws but rather attempts to discover a consensus among users of financial information. Since the accounting process is an artifically created mathematical model of an entity, there is heavy reliance on *authoritative support* in determining the principles and procedures used to implement the accounting model.

Rule 203 of the AICPA's Code of Professional Ethics clearly designates the principles contained in pronouncements of the FASB and its predecessors as generally accepted accounting principles. Pronouncements covered by Rule 203 include: FASB Statements and Interpretations, Accounting Research Bulletins, and APB Opinions. The Code of Professional Ethics and Rule 203 are discussed in detail in Chapter 3.

The pronouncements covered by Rule 203 are by definition sufficient authoritative support. When these pronouncements are silent on an issue, the practitioner is faced with the problem of determining a hierarchy of authority within the accounting literature and determining how much authoritative support is sufficient or substantial.

Substantial authoritative support is directly dependent upon the quality of support for a particular accounting principle. The researcher must know the hierarchy of authority and make a determination as to whether the support found for a particular accounting principle is sufficient to include the principle in GAAP. The heirarchy is not well-defined for authoritative bodies other than the FASB and its predecessors, but certain criteria can be used to identify authoritative groups. The APB subcommittee on the project entitled "Basic Concepts and Broad Accounting Principles" delineated an authoritative group as a body composed of informed, intelligent, and experienced accountants. Presumably, the practitioner can look to professional and governmental standard-setting groups to meet the criteria.

The AICPA is the primary national professional organization for certified public accountants. The various publications of the Institute are the result of informed and thoughtful deliberations of experienced accountants. The AICPA Industry Accounting Guides and Statements of Position are given a high degree of authority. Many practitioners follow these AICPA guidelines as closely as official pronouncements of the FASB even though Rule 203 of the Code of Professional Ethics does not require such adherence.

The Securities and Exchange Commission does not have as broad a sphere of authority as the FASB, but its influence is pervasive. The corporations that control the majority of the nation's capital assets are "publicly held," and these corporations are subject to the regulations of the SEC. Thus the Commission has legal authority over the accounting principles used by the major corporations in this country. The SEC has generally delegated the responsibility for establishing GAAP to the private sector, namely the AICPA and FASB. However, the SEC reporting requirements must be adhered to by companies which are required to file reports with the Commission.

The researcher may be confronted with an issue that has not been specifically addressed by any of the authoritative bodies previously mentioned. In such a case, there are secondary sources which will contribute to substantial authoritative support for an accounting principle but of themselves are not sufficient. These secondary sources are listed in Figure 2-1, which summarizes the major sources of accounting authoritative support.

Summary

This chapter presented an overview of the accounting standard-setting environment and the accounting standard-setting process. The primary organizations impacting the standard-setting process include the FASB, AICPA, SEC, CASB, and NCGA. The researcher should be cognizant of these organizations and the authority of their official publications.

Figure 2-1

ACCOUNTING AUTHORITATIVE SUPPORT

Primary Authoritative Support

Sources which provide sufficient authoritative support for including a particular accounting principle within GAAP.

A. General Application to the Field of Accounting
   1. FASB Statements of Financial Accounting Standards
   2. FASB Interpretations
   3. Opinions of the Accounting Principles Board
   4. Accounting Research Bulletins of the Committee on Accounting Procedures

B. Special Application to Certain Entities
   1. AICPA Industry Accounting Guides
   2. AICPA Statements of Position
   3. Regulations of the Securities and Exchange Commission
   4. Statements of the Cost Accounting Standards Board
   5. Interpretations of the Cost Accounting Standards Board
   6. Statements of the National Council on Governmental Accounting

Secondary Authoritative Support

Sources which support inclusion of particular accounting principles within GAAP, but individually are not sufficient authoritative support;
   1. Substantial industrial practice
   2. Pronouncements of industry regulatory authorities
   3. Published research studies of authoritative professional and industrial societies
   4. Publications of recognized industry associations
   5. Accounting research monographs of the AICPA
   6. Accounting textbooks and reference books authored by recognized authorities in the field

DISCUSSION QUESTIONS

1. Discuss the environmental factors that influence the standard setting process.
2. What appears to be an underlying reason for the establishment of accounting standards?
3. Identify the authoritative accounting pronouncements of the AICPA and FASB.
4. Describe the rule-making or due-process procedures of the FASB in the establishment of a standard.
5. What is the FASB's Conceptual Framework Project? Of what benefit is this Project to the practitioner?
6. Identify the authoritative publications of the SEC, CASB, and NCGA.
7. What constitutes generally accepted accounting principles?
8. What is meant by the term "authoritative support"?
9. What are the implications of GAAP and authoritative support to the researcher?
10. Distinguish between primary authoritative support and secondary authoritative support.

Chapter 3

THE ENVIRONMENT OF
AUDITING RESEARCH AND
PROFESSIONAL JUDGMENT

The role of the independent auditor can be described as a secondary communication function, whereby the auditor expresses an opinion on the financial information reported by management. A primary concern of the auditor is whether the client's financial statements are presented in accordance with generally accepted accounting principles. In addition, the auditor must be concerned with the auditing standards and procedures and the professional ethics that must be followed in the conduct of an audit. These standards, procedures, and ethics are the focus of auditing research.

In conducting an examination of financial statements, the auditor makes tests of the accounting records which he or she considers necessary in order to obtain sufficient evidence to render an opinion. Choosing the accounting records to examine and deciding upon the extent to which they should be examined are strictly matters for the auditor's professional judgment. Indeed, many auditing pronouncements explicitly or implicitly state the need for the exercise of professional judgment in the examination of financial statements.

The objective of this chapter is to present an overview of the auditing standard-setting environment, the auditing standard-setting process, and the role of professional judgment in the research process.

Auditing Standard-Setting Environment

In a complex society, where credit is extended widely and business failures occur daily, and where investors wish to study the financial statements of many enterprises, the role of auditing is indispensable. The purpose of the audit report is to lend credibility to the financial information.

The early development of auditing standards and procedures in the U. S. can be traced to significant economic events and circumstances. In 1917 the Federal Reserve Board issued the first audit guideline, entitled "A Memorandum on Balance Sheet Audits." This publication was a result of the credit problems of businesses during the early 1900s. Later, the stock market crash and the ensuing depression led to the creation of the Securities and Exchange Commission and prompted the New York Stock Exchange to require that listed companies be audited. Throughout these years, the AICPA was actively involved in the development of auditing standards and procedures.

Auditing Standards

Auditing standards differ from auditing procedures in that standards provide measures of the quality of performance, whereas audit procedures refer to the acts or steps to be performed in an engagement. Auditing standards do not vary. They remain the same for all audits. However, auditing procedures change depending on the nature and type of entity under audit and the complexity of the audit.

In contrast to generally accepted accounting principles, which cannot be identified with exactness, the AICPA has formally adopted ten broad requirements for auditors to follow in examining financial statements. These ten requirements are referred to as the ten *generally accepted auditing standards (GAAS)* and are as follows:

General Standards
1. The examination is to be performed by a person or persons having adequate technical training and proficiency as an auditor.
2. In all matters relating to the assignment, an independence in mental attitude is to be maintained by the auditor or auditors.
3. Due professional care is to be exercised in the performance of the examination and the preparation of the report.

Standards of Field Work
1. The work is to be adequately planned and assistants, if any, are to be properly supervised.
2. There is to be a proper study and evaluation of the existing internal control as a basis for reliance thereon and for the determination of the resultant extent of the tests to which auditing procedures are to be restricted.
3. Sufficient competent evidential matter is to be obtained through inspection, observation, inquiries, and confirmations to afford a reasonable basis for an opinion regarding the financial statements under examination.

Standards of Reporting
1. The report shall state whether the financial statements are presented in accordance with generally accepted principles of accounting.
2. The report shall state whether such principles have been consistently observed in the current period in relation to the preceding period.
3. Informative disclosures in the financial statements are to be regarded as reasonably adequate unless otherwise stated in the report.
4. The report shall contain either an expression of opinion regarding the financial statements, taken as a whole, or an assertion to the effect that an opinion cannot be expressed. When an overall opinion cannot be expressed, the reasons therefor should be stated. In all cases where an auditor's name is associated with financial statements, the report should contain a clear-cut indication of the character of the auditor's examination, if any, and the degree of responsibility he or she is taking.

In addition to the issuance of the generally accepted auditing standards, the AICPA publishes a series of *Statements on Auditing Standards.* These statements supplement and interpret the ten generally accepted standards by clarifying audit procedures or prescribing the form and content of the auditor's report.

Various forms of the generally accepted auditing standards are recognized by governmental and internal auditors. The General Accounting Office (GAO), through the comptroller general of the United States, has issued *Standards for Audit of Governmental Organizations, Programs, Activities and Functions.* This pamphlet identifies auditing standards for governmental auditors. The Institute of Internal Auditors has issued *Standards for the Professional Practice of Internal Auditing* under which internal auditors operate.

Auditing Standard-Setting Process

Concern has always existed as to who should set auditing standards for the independent auditor. Prior to the establishment of the SEC, Congress had considered having audits conducted by a corps of governmental auditors. However, federal chartering of auditors did not take place, and to this day the auditing standard-setting process for independent audits remains in the private sector under the auspices of the

AICPA's present senior technical committee on auditing standards — the Auditing Standards Board.

The establishment and issuance of auditing standards has traditionally been the responsibility of the AICPA. Its Committee on Auditing Procedure (CAP) was formed on January 30, 1939, and issued a series of *Statements on Auditing Procedure*. These statements were to serve as guidelines for the independent auditor in the exercise of professional judgment on the application of auditing procedures. This committee functioned from 1939-1972 and issued 54 statements.

In November, 1972, the Statements on Auditing Procedure were codified in *Statement on Auditing Standards No. 1*, "Codification of Auditing Standards and Procedures." At this time, the AICPA reorganized its auditing section and changed the name of the committee to the Auditing Standards Executive Committee (AudSEC) and created the Auditing Standards Division within the AICPA. AudSEC served as the AICPA's senior technical committee with the charge of interpreting generally accepted auditing standards and responsibility for issuing Statements on Auditing Standards (SASs).

As a result of the recommendations of the Commission on Auditors' Responsibilities — an independent study group appointed by the AICPA in 1974 to study the structure of the auditing standard-setting process — the AICPA in May, 1978, restructured its auditing committee. In October, 1978, a 15-member Auditing Standards Board (ASB) was formed as the successor to AudSEC on all auditing matters and is the present body authorized to issue Statements on Auditing Standards. The Board was given the following charge:

> The AICPA Auditing Standards Board shall be responsible for the promulgation of auditing standards and procedures to be observed by members of the AICPA in accordance with the Institute's rules of conduct.
>
> The board shall be alert to new opportunities for auditors to serve the public, both by the assumption of new responsibilities and by improved ways of meeting old ones, and shall as expeditiously as possible develop standards and procedures that will enable the auditor to assume those responsibilities.
>
> Auditing standards and procedures promulgated by the board shall:
>
> a. Define the nature and extent of the auditor's responsibilities.
> b. Provide guidance to the auditor in carrying out his duties, enabling him to express an opinion on the reliability of the representations on which he is reporting.
> c. Make special provision, where appropriate, to meet the needs of small enterprises.
> d. Have regard to the costs which they impose on society in relation to the benefits reasonably expected to be derived from the audit function.
>
> The auditing standards board shall provide auditors with all possible guidance in the implementation of its pronouncements, by means of

interpretations of its statements, by the issuance of guidelines, and by other means available to it.[1]

In addition, the staff of the Auditing Standards Division has been authorized to issue auditing interpretations as to the application of pronouncements (SASs) of the Auditing Standards Board. The interpretations are not to be considered as authoritative as a Statement on Auditing Standards. However, members need to be aware that they may have to justify any departure from an interpretation issued by the Auditing Standards Division of the AICPA. Other publications of the Auditing Standards Division include a number of Industry Audit Guides and Statements of Position. Figure 3-1 presents an overview of the current sources of authoritative auditing support. The auditor should be aware of each of the sources listed, particularly the Statements on Auditing Standards.

Figure 3-1

AUDITING AUTHORITATIVE SUPPORT

Primary Authoritative Support

   A. General Application
      1. Statements on Auditing Standards
      2. Auditing Interpretations
      3. AICPA Code of Ethics

   B. Special Application to Certain Entities
      1. Industry Audit Guides
      2. Statements of Position of the Auditing Standards Division
      3. GAO Standards for governmental audits

Secondary Authoritative Support

   A. Audit Research Monographs
   B. AICPA Audit and Accounting Manual
   C. Journal articles and textbooks

The current standard-setting process of the ASB is somewhat similar to that of the FASB:

1. A specific auditing problem or issue is identified.
2. A task force may be established to conduct research on the problem or issue.

---

[1]*AICPA Professional Standards*, Volume 1 (Chicago: Commerce Clearing House), Appendix A.

3. Public meetings are held to discuss the auditing issue.
4. An exposure draft of a proposed Statement on Auditing Standards may be issued for public comment.
5. A final pronouncement, Statement on Auditing Standards, is issued.

Code of Professional Ethics

A hallmark of a profession is the establishment of a code of ethics that governs the conduct of its members. The AICPA Code of Professional Ethics consists of four major parts:

1. Concepts of Professional Ethics
2. Rules of Conduct
3. Interpretations of Rules of Conduct
4. Ethics Rulings

The concepts consist of five broad statements relating to the conduct every CPA should strive for. They constitute the philosophical foundation for the Rules of Conduct. These Rules of Conduct set forth minimum guidelines for the ethical conduct of members of the AICPA.

The AICPA's committee on professional ethics has issued a number of Interpretations of Rules of Conduct to assist members in their attempt to resolve ethical problems. These Interpretations provide guidance in the determination of the scope and applicability of the Rules.

The committee also issues Ethics Rulings which explain the applicability of the Rules of Conduct and Interpretations to specific situations. Ethics Rulings are issued in response to inquiries by members concerning specific cases.

Rules of Conduct are mandatory and enforceable. Any departure from these rules may result in disciplinary action. Departures from Interpretations and Ethics Rulings may also result in disciplinary action unless the departure can be justified in the circumstances. Disciplinary action may lead to suspension or termination of AICPA membership. Further, a violation of professional ethics may result in revocation of a CPA's certificate or license to practice by a state board of accountancy.

The AICPA's Code of Professional Ethics applies to all members. Certain rules, however, are specifically applicable to the independent auditor. Rule 202, which requires compliance with the ten generally accepted auditing standards and the Statements on Auditing Standards, is stated as follows:

Rule 202 — Auditing standards. A member shall not permit his name to be associated with financial statements in such a manner as to imply that he is acting as an independent public accountant unless he has complied with the applicable generally accepted auditing standards promulgated by the Institute. Statements on auditing standards issued by the Institute's auditing standards board are, for purposes of this rule, considered to be interpretations of the generally accepted auditing standards, and departures from such statements must be justified by those who do not follow them.[2]

Rule 203 generally prohibits the auditor from expressing an opinion that financial statements are in conformity with generally accepted accounting principles if the statements contain any departure from the official pronouncements of the Financial Accounting Standards Board or its predecessors. Rule 203 is stated as follows:

Rule 203 — Accounting principles. A member shall not express an opinion that financial statements are presented in conformity with generally accepted accounting principles if such statements contain any departure from an accounting principle promulgated by the body designated by Council to establish such principles which has a material effect on the statements taken as a whole, unless the member can demonstrate that due to unusual circumstances the financial statements would otherwise have been misleading. In such cases his report must describe the departure, the approximate effects thereof, if practicable, and the reasons why compliance with the principle would result in a misleading statement.[3]

Rule 203 was clarified with the issuance of the following three Interpretations:

Interpretations under Rule 203 — Accounting principles

203-1 — Departures from established accounting principles. Rule 203 was adopted to require compliance with accounting principles promulgated by the body designated by Council to establish such principles. There is a strong presumption that adherence to officially established accounting principles would in nearly all instances result in financial statements that are not misleading.

However, in the establishment of accounting principles it is difficult to anticipate all of the circumstances to which such principles might be applied. This rule therefore recognizes that upon occasion there may be unusual circumstances where the literal application of pronouncements on accounting principles would have the effect of rendering financial statements misleading. In such cases, the proper accounting treatment is that which will render the financial statements not misleading.

The question of what constitutes unusual circumstances as referred to in Rule 203 is a matter of professional judgment involving the ability to support the position that adherence to a promulgated principle would be regarded generally by reasonable men as producing a misleading result.

Examples of events which may justify departures from a principle are new legislation or the evolution of a new form of business transaction. An unusual degree of materiality or the existence of conflicting industry practices are examples of circumstances which would not ordinarily be regarded as unusual in the context of Rule 203.

---

[2]*AICPA Professional Standards,* Volume 2 (Chicago: Commerce Clearing House), ET Section 202.

[3]*Ibid,* ET Section 203.

203-2 — Status of FASB interpretations. Council is authorized under Rule 203 to designate a body to establish accounting principles and has designated the Financial Accounting Standards Board as such body. Council also has resolved that FASB Statements of Financial Accounting Standards, together with those Accounting Research Bulletins and APB Opinions which are not superseded by action of the FASB, constitute accounting principles as contemplated in Rule 203.

In determining the existence of a departure from an accounting principle established by a Statement of Financial Accounting Standards, Accounting Research Bulletin or APB Opinion encompassed by Rule 203, the division of professional ethics will construe such Statement, Bulletin or Opinion in the light of any interpretations thereof issued by the FASB.

203-3 — FASB statements that establish standards for disclosure outside of the basic financial statements. The Council resolution designating the Financial Accounting Standards Board as the body to establish accounting principles pursuant to Rule 203 through the issuance of Statements of Financial Accounting Standards relates solely to the provisions of Statements of Financial Accounting Standards (SFASs) which established accounting principles with respect to basic financial statements (balance sheets, statements of income, statements of changes in retained earnings, disclosures of changes in other categories of stockholder's equity, statements of changes in financial position, and descriptions of accounting policies and related notes).

SFASs which stipulate that certain information should be disclosed outside the basic financial statements are not covered by Rule 203.[4]

Role of Judgment in Accounting and Auditing Research

Judgment is prevalent throughout accounting and auditing. The accountant or auditor exercises professional judgment in considering whether the substance of business transactions differs from the form, in evaluating the adequacy of disclosure, assessing the probable impact of future events, and determining materiality limits.

The review of current authoritative literature reveals that certain pronouncements on generally accepted accounting principles disclose specifically which accounting principle is applicable for a given business transaction. Other pronouncements only provide general guidelines for their application and in some cases suggest acceptable alternative principles. The process of applying professional judgment in choosing among alternatives is not carried out in isolation, but through consultation with other professionals knowledgeable in the area.

Statement on Auditing Standards No. 5 makes the following point on the use of professional judgment in determining conformity with GAAP:

---

[4]*Ibid.*

.04 The auditor's opinion that financial statements present fairly an entity's financial position, results of operations, and changes in financial position in conformity with generally accepted accounting principles *should be based on his judgment* as to whether

(a) the accounting principles selected and applied have general acceptance;

(b) the accounting principles are appropriate in the circumstances;

(c) the financial statements, including the related notes, are informative of matters that may affect their use, understanding, and interpretation;

(d) the information presented in the financial statements is classified and summarized in a reasonable manner, that is, neither too detailed nor too condensed; and

(e) the financial statements reflect the underlying events and transactions in a manner that presents the financial position, results of operations, and changes in financial position stated within a range of acceptable limits, that is, limits that are reasonable and practicable to attain in financial statements. (Emphasis added)[5]

In an attempt to render an opinion based upon professional judgment, the auditor often considers the opinions of other professionals. In such a case, there are several published sources the practitioner can use to determine how others have dealt with specific accounting and reporting applications of GAAP. The AICPA publishes *Technical Practice Aids* which contains the "Technical Information Service." This service consists of inquiries and replies which describe an actual problem that was encountered in practice and the interpretation and recommendations that were provided along with relevant standards and other authoritative sources. Chapter 5 includes a detailed discussion of *Technical Practice Aids*.

The AICPA also provides other reference sources for the practitioner to use in determining the current state of the art in applying accounting principles. *Accounting Trends & Techniques* is an annual publication designed to illustrate current reporting practices and chart significant trends in these practices. *Financial Reporting Surveys* is a continuing series of studies designed to show in detail how specific accounting and reporting questions are actually being handled. The National Automated Accounting Research System (NAARS) is a full-text, computer-based information retrieval system maintained by the AICPA. Among the information stored by this system are the annual reports of over 4,000 publicly traded corporations. These research tools are discussed in detail in Chapter 6. The practitioner can use these references to determine current accounting and reporting practices. With the use of information gathered and through consultation with other accountants, a

---

[5]*Ibid*, Volume 1, AU Section 411.04.

decision may be reached on the appropriate accounting principle to be used for the transaction being researched or the auditing issue under investigation.

Summary

This chapter has presented an overview of the auditing standard-setting environment with discussions of the auditing standard-setting process and professional ethics. Familiarity with this information will aid the auditor in the auditing research process.

In researching an accounting or auditing issue, the practitioner may be called upon to use professional judgment in the decision-making process. Experience is undoubtedly the primary factor in developing good professional judgment. However, the subsequent chapters present a research methodology that should aid in the development of professional judgment.

DISCUSSION QUESTIONS

1. Identify major factors that have resulted in the establishment of auditing standards.
2. Differentiate between auditing standards and auditing procedures.
3. Discuss the relationship between generally accepted auditing standards (GAAS) and Statements on Auditing Standards (SAS).
4. Discuss the applicability of the first and third general standards of GAAS to accounting and auditing research.
5. What standards are issued for governmental and internal auditors?
6. Discuss the historical relationship of the Auditing Standards Board, Auditing Standards Executive Committee, and the Committee on Auditing Procedure. Also, list the authoritative pronouncements issued by each body.
7. Explain the importance of the Code of Professional Ethics in the conduct of an audit.
8. Explain the significance of Rules 202 and 203 of the AICPA's Code of Professional Ethics.
9. What role does professional judgment play in the daily activities of the accountant or auditor?

Chapter 4

EXPANDING THE
RESEARCH PROCESS

This chapter focuses on the four basic research steps introduced in Chapter 1 and expands upon the application of those steps by applying them to an illustrative problem. Since the emphasis in the chapter is on the research process, the illustration will use only the *FASB Accounting Standards* series as the source of authoritative literature. Detailed discussion of this series and other publications that can be used in the research process is deferred until the next chapter.

Method of Conducting Research

The foundation for practical accounting and auditing research has now been set. The practitioner will generally be confronted with problems relating to the proper accounting treatment for given transactions or the proper financial presentation of accounting data and disclosure requirements. The focus of the research will be to determine the appropriate alternative principles, locate authoritative support for these alternatives, and apply professional judgment in selecting one principle from the list of alternatives. What the researcher now needs is a systematic method to conduct research in the most efficient and effective manner.

The following problem is designed to highlight the research steps introduced in Chapter 1, with emphasis on the use of the *FASB Account-*

ing Standards Current Text. This example will be used for the remainder
of the chapter to help explain the four basic research steps.

John Remis owns a manufacturing company, Remis Products
Inc., which stamps steel parts used in various home appliances.
Remis has been the sole shareholder of the company for several
years and has developed good customer accounts with several
companies producing major home appliances. These customers
have urged Remis to expand his operations to produce more parts
and to assemble subcomponents for various appliances. He has
been assured that there will be a good market for the additional
parts and components and has decided to expand operations.
Remis has explored several possibilities for financing the plant
expansion required for the new operations. He has decided to
obtain the necessary capital by selling shares of Remis Products to
the public. Since audited financial statements are required in con-
nection with a public offering of securities, Remis has engaged a
CPA to audit the company's statements for the first time. In reviewing the accounting procedures used by Remis Products, the CPA
discovers that inventories are recorded at their direct costs with-
out regard to factory overhead costs. Factory overhead represents
20 percent of the total manufacturing cost of the units produced,
and inventories represent approximately 55 percent of current assets. The CPA performing the audit questions the procedure of
excluding overhead from inventory costs.

Step 1—Identify the Issue or Problem. Identification of the issue
or problem is a critical step in the research process and one that is
too often given the least attention. This step can be subdivided into
three components:

1. Preliminary problem identification
2. Problem analysis
3. Refined statement of the problem

Preliminary problem identification simply means that a potential
problem must be recognized before any action will be taken to solve it.
Timely resolution of potential problems is crucial to an efficient audit.
If an accounting problem is recognized late in the audit engagement,
the research may be conducted hastily and inefficiently due to time
pressures, thus increasing the danger of an erroneous conclusion. Also,
failure to identify potential problems in the early stages of an audit may
result in the need for additional tests and procedures which could increase the overall cost of the audit.

The auditor is more likely to identify and resolve problems on a
timely basis if he or she has a working knowledge of all AICPA and
FASB standards and is familiar with statements from other authoritative

sources. Also, the auditor should maintain year-round contact with continuing audit clients to keep abreast of new business transactions or changes in the business environment that would affect their financial statements. This will result in early detection of potential problems. Analytical review procedures conducted early in the audit engagement can also reveal potential problem areas.

A problem generally arises because a company is involved in new business transactions, or new pronouncements have been issued requiring the application of different accounting standards. In the example, the desire of Remis to sell stock in a public offering and the requirement of an audit have resulted in the identification of an accounting problem by the auditor. The preliminary problem statement in this case could be:

> The company is recording inventories at direct costs without regard to factory overhead.

Once the auditor becomes aware of a potential problem, he or she must analyze the nature of the transaction or event that has caused the problem and determine the economic impact on all parties involved. This step generally encompasses a review of underlying records and documents and interviews with appropriate personnel.

Analysis of the potential problem presented in the example reveals the following:

1. As a result of excluding overhead from inventory costs—
   a. Inventories may be understated on the balance sheet by a material amount.
   b. Net income for the current period may be understated by a material amount.
2. If the current inventory pricing method is not in conformity with generally accepted accounting principles, the company must change to an acceptable method in order for the auditor to express an unqualified opinion on the financial statements.
3. A change in the inventory pricing method would alter the trend of earnings reported by the company and could result in an increased tax liability for the company.

The final stage of Step 1 is the refined statement of the problem. If the researcher states the problem inaccurately, the remaining research steps can be properly conducted but the conclusion may be inappropriate. Incomplete or erroneous problem definition results in costly, inefficient research.

The refined statement of the problem should be written in simple terms that address all important aspects of the situation and in terms that identify the key accounting concepts. These concepts can then be used in the search of the professional literature. In the example, a refined statement of the problem could be written as follows:

Is exclusion of overhead acceptable in inventory pricing and, if not, how should the change from an erroneous accounting procedure to a generally accepted procedure be reported in the financial statements?

Step 2 — Collect Evidence. The collection of evidence generally involves: (1) a review of related accounting or auditing literature and (2) a survey of present practice.

Review of Accounting or Auditing Literature. The review of the literature should begin with the pronouncements of official standard-setting bodies — generally the FASB and AICPA or, in certain cases, the SEC, CASB, or NCGA. It is important to note the scope of any pronouncements reviewed. Time should not be spent in a detailed review of pronouncements that are not applicable to the transaction under investigation. Pronouncements that do not specifically address the research problem, but are related to it, should not be completely ignored. They can be reviewed for possible references to other appropriate sources, or discussions within these pronouncements can add insights into the problem at hand. If these primary sources do not provide the needed accounting or auditing information, then the search must extend to secondary authoritative sources such as industrial practices, published research studies, and other relevant sources.

A list of keywords is essential to locating relevant authoritative literature. The reader should note that a good problem statement will generate the initial keywords necessary to access the appropriate sections of the professional literature. After the search has begun, additional keywords may be identified.

From the refined statement of the problem in the example, the following keywords can be identified:

> Overhead
> Inventory pricing
> Accounting changes

With these keywords as a starting point, the Topical Index of the *FASB Accounting Standards — Current Text* can be used to locate relevant sections.

Keyword	References
Overhead	No relevant references
Inventory Pricing —	
Overhead	I78.106
Accounting Changes —	
Inventory Cost Elements	A06.108
Inventory Pricing-Change in Method	A06.107-.108; A06.112; A06.122-.123
Types of Changes	A06.104-.107; A06.111-.116

Inventory Pricing. Section I78.106, referenced under Inventory Pricing—Overhead, states in part, "Exclusion of all overheads from inventory costs does not constitute an accepted accounting procedure." The official pronouncement cited is Accounting Research Bulletin No. 43, Chapter 4, paragraph 5.

Accounting Changes. Sections A06.107 states that "a change in the method of inventory pricing" is an example of a change in accounting principle. The following paragraph, A06.108, states, "A change in composition of the elements of cost included in inventory also is an accounting change..." which should be reported as a change in principle. The original pronouncements cited are APB Opinion No. 20, paragraph 9 (A06.107) and FASB Interpretation No. 1, paragraph 9 (A06.108). These two sections suggest that a change in inventory pricing methods by Remis Products is an "accounting change" which should be reported as a "change in accounting principle."

The researcher, however, should continue the literature search until all relevant references have been reviewed. Sections A06.105-.106 indicate that a "change in accounting principle" involves a change from one generally accepted principle to another (APB Opinion No. 20, paragraphs 7 and 8). Since Remis is changing from an erroneous method to one that is generally accepted, the change is not a change in principle. Section A06.104, which defines "accounting changes," states that the correction of an error is not an accounting change (APB Opinion No. 20, paragraph 6).

As noted previously, additional keywords may be identified in the course of the literature search. From the review of the literature referenced under "Accounting Changes," the keyword "Errors" or "Error Correction" is identified.

Errors. Under "Errors and Irregularities," the following references are found in the Topical Index.

Errors or Irregularities
Disclosure Requirements, Corrections.......................A35.105
Distinguished from Accounting Changes.....................A06.104; A35.104
Examples..A35.104
Prior Period Adjustments A35.103; A35.105
Reporting Corrections A35.104

Section A35.104 states, "A change from an accounting principle that is not generally accepted to one that is generally accepted is a correction of an error for purposes of applying this section." The source cited is APB Opinion No. 20, paragraph 13. Section A35.103 states that a correction of an error is to be accounted for and reported as a prior period adjustment (FASB Statement No. 16, paragraph 11). Specific disclosure requirements are set fourth in Sections A35.105-.107.

Survey of Present Practice. In addition to the review of authoritative literature, Step 2 involves determining how other companies with similar circumstances or transactions have handled the accounting and reporting procedures. This survey could include a review of *Accounting Trends & Techniques, Financial Reporting Surveys,* or a National Automated Accounting Research System (NAARS) computer search (discussed in detail in Chapter 6).

Step 3 — Evaluate Results and Identify Alternatives. This step requires the exercise of professional judgment. The evidence should be carefully reviewed and one or more tentative conclusions identified. The quality and amount of authoritative support for each alternative should be evaluated. Also, the evidence may be reviewed with other accountants knowledgeable in the field.

In the example the key issue is whether the change in the inventory costing method is a change in accounting principle or a correction of an error. The proper accounting treatment hinges on this question. *APB Opinion No. 20,* "Accounting Changes," addresses this issue and clearly defines this problem as a correction of an error.

Step 4 — Develop Conclusion. If the evaluation process is properly performed, the researcher should be able to develop a well-reasoned, well-supported conclusion as to the appropriate resolution of the problem. In the illustrative problem, the change is a correction of an error which should be reported as a prior period adjustment. The correction should be made retroactively for all accounts affected. Disclosure should be made of the effects on income before extraordinary items, net income, and per share amounts. Since no amounts were indicated in this problem, the restated financial statements and disclosures are not given.

Documenting the Research Process

Thorough documentation is a crucial part of the entire research process. The documentation should include a statement of the problem and relevant facts; references to authoritative literature used; a description of alternative procedures considered and the authoritative support for each alternative; and an explanation of why certain alternatives were discarded and why the recommended principle or procedure was selected.

A *research memorandum* is often used to summarize the research. A file of such memoranda can be maintained for future reference so that time will not be wasted analyzing problems previously researched. Following is a research memorandum that could be written to document the example problem.

Research Memorandum
Regarding Initial Audit of Remis Products Inc.
From — Audit Supervisor

Remis Products Inc. is a new client that has requested an audit for the purpose of a public offering of securities to raise capital for expansion. It was discovered that Remis excludes overhead from the cost of inventories. Research was conducted to determine the acceptability of this procedure for financial statement presentation. A literature search was conducted in order to determine whether a change in inventory pricing procedures would be necessary in order for the financial statements to conform to GAAP.

The problem researched was, "Is exclusion of overhead acceptable in inventory pricing and, if not, how should the change from an erroneous accounting procedure to a generally accepted procedure be reported in the financial statements?"

If the client's procedure is erroneous, the inventories presented on the current and prior periods' balance sheets are materially understated. Also, net income for the current period is understated by a material amount. If the present method is not in conformity with GAAP, a change in methods is required in order for the auditor to express an unqualified opinion on the financial statements. A change in inventory pricing methods to include overhead in inventory costs will change reported earnings and will result in an initial increase in the company's tax liability.

The key sections examined in the literature review are as follows:
1. "Exclusion of all overheads from inventory costs does not constitute an acceptable accounting procedure" (ARB No. 43, ch. 4, par. 5).
2. "A change from an accounting principle that is not generally accepted to one that is generally accepted is a correction of an error" (APB Opinion No. 20, par. 13).
3. "Correction of an error in the financial statements of a prior period" is to be "accounted for and reported" as a prior period adjustment" (FASB Statement No. 16, par. 11).

Therefore, based upon the research, Remis Products is incorrectly pricing inventory. The correction of this erroneous pricing procedure should be considered as a correction of an error which should be handled as a prior period adjustment. The correction should be made retroactively for all periods presented. Disclosure of the effects on income before extraordinary items, net income, and per share amounts should be reported.

Summary

This chapter has provided an overview of the four basic steps in the research process. The simple example was used to illustrate these steps and to describe in detail how each step is applied to a specific situation. Figure 4-1 summarizes these four steps and lists the specific components of each step.

Figure 4-1

THE RESEARCH PROCESS

Basic Steps in Research Process	Specific Components
1. Define the issue or problem	a. Preliminary problem identification b. Problem analysis c. Refined statement of the problem
2. Collect evidence Review related literature	a. Identification of keywords to be used in the literature search b. Review of appropriate citations
Survey present practice	a. Review of publications or computer-based services b. Consultation with other professionals
3. Evaluate results and identify alternatives	a. Identification of alternative principles or procedures b. Evaluation of authoritative support for the alternatives identified c. Consultation with other professionals
4. Develop conclusion	a. Selection of the appropriate principle or procedure b. Preparation of memo summarizing the research process, results, and the conclusion and underlying support or justification

---

Chapters 5 and 6 focus on techniques for accessing the authoritative literature, and Chapter 7 presents a comprehensive problem encompassing the details of the entire research process.

Chapter **5**

SOURCES OF
AUTHORITATIVE LITERATURE

A major component of the research process is the review of the pertinent accounting or auditing literature. This chapter outlines the overall structure of the authoritative literature with an emphasis on developing the technical skills required to access the *AICPA Professional Standards* and the *FASB Accounting Standards* series, which are the most comprehensive sources of authoritative accounting and auditing literature.

Many of the techniques, such as the keyword index, used to access the AICPA or the FASB Standards series are also applicable to pronouncements of other rule-making bodies. In addition to the AICPA and the FASB, the Cost Accounting Standards Board (CASB), the National Council on Governmental Accounting (NCGA), and the Securities and Exchange Commission (SEC) produce publications stating their official positions on various accounting issues. The AICPA, FASB, and the SEC also publish unofficial interpretations and descriptive surveys to help the practitioner implement required accounting principles. The identification and use of these unofficial publications are also discussed.

Sources of Authoritative Literature

Many research sources are available to aid the researcher in the quest for a solution to a particular problem or issue. A summary of the various sources of authoritative literature on accounting principles and auditing standards follows.

1. Pronouncements of authoritative bodies that prescribe accounting principles which must be followed in order for the financial statements to be considered in conformity with generally accepted accounting principles.

Authoritative Body	Name of Publication
AICPA—	
Committee on Accounting Procedures	Accounting Research Bulletins
Committee on Terminology	Accounting Terminology Bulletins
Accounting Principles Board (APB)	APB Opinions
Cost Accounting Standards Board	Cost Accounting Standards Interpretations
Financial Accounting Standards Board	Statements of Financial Accounting Standards Interpretations
Municipal Finance Officers' Association—	
National Committee on Governmental Accounting	Governmental Accounting, Auditing and Financial Reporting
National Council on Governmental Accounting	Statements
Securities and Exchange Commission	Regulation S-K Regulation S-X Accounting Series Releases Financial Reporting Releases Accounting and Auditing Enforcement Releases

2. Authoritative literature that is considered descriptive of generally accepted accounting principles, but does not prescribe such principles.

Authoritative Body	Name of Publication
AICPA—	
Special Committees	Industry Accounting Guides
Accounting Standards Division	Statements of Position

3. Literature which unofficially interprets pronouncements of authoritative bodies.

Authoritative Body	Name of Publication
AICPA — Accounting Principles Board	APB Interpretations
Financial Accounting Standards Board	Technical Bulletins
Securities and Exchange Commission	Staff Accounting Bulletins

4. Authoritative literature which expresses views on accounting theory rather than specific elements of generally accepted accounting principles.

Authoritative Body	Name of Publication
AICPA — Accounting Principles Board	APB Statements
Financial Accounting Standards Board	Statements of Financial Accounting Concepts

5. Authoritative literature on auditing standards.

Authoritative Body	Name of Publication
AICPA— Auditing Standards Division	Statements on Auditing Standards Auditing Interpretations Industry Audit Guides Statements of Position
Professional Ethics Division	Code of Professional Ethics

Accessing the Authoritative Literature

As can be seen from the previous section, there are many sources of authoritative accounting and auditing literature. The publications presented in Figure 5-1 are among the researcher's most valuable tools for identifying and locating authoritative literature in the specific area under investigation. These research services enable the practitioner to keep abreast of the pronouncements, interpretations, and guidelines that govern today's technical and professional activities. The publications and techniques for using them to conduct efficient research are discussed in the following sections.

Index to Accounting and Auditing Technical Pronouncements This guide, published annually by the staff of the AICPA, is designed to meet

Figure 5-1 — PRIMARY RESEARCH PUBLICATIONS

Index to pronouncements of the AICPA, FASB, SEC, and other professional and regulatory bodies.

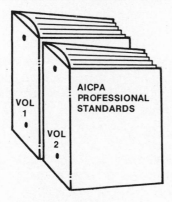

- U.S. Auditing Standards
- Accounting and Review Services
- Code of Professional Ethics
- AICPA Bylaws
- International Accounting
- International Auditing
- Management Advisory Services
- Quality Control
- Tax Practice

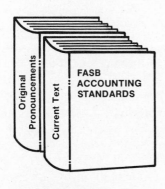

- FASB Statements, Interpretations, and Technical Bulletins
- APB Opinions, Statements, and Interpretations
- Accounting Research Bulletins
- Accounting Terminology Bulletins

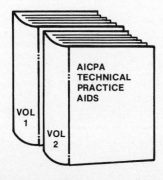

- Technical Information Service
- Statements of Position of the Accounting Standards Division
- Statements of Position of the Auditing Standards Division
- Voluntary Quality Control Review Program

the need for an efficient reference to current accounting and auditing standards. It provides a cumulative index of both authoritative and semi-authoritative sources of accounting and auditing pronouncements. It is intended to provide access to the pronouncements of the following authoritative bodies:

1. American Institute of Certified Public Accountants
2. Cost Accounting Standards Board
3. Financial Accounting Standards Board
4. International Accounting Standards Committee
5. International Federation of Accountants
6. Municipal Finance Officers' Association
7. National Council on Governmental Accounting
8. Securities and Exchange Commission

The index is designed to coordinate the retrieval of information from all sources of accounting and auditing technical pronouncements. The index aids efficient research in that it provides a quick reference to official pronouncements of many authoritative bodies. Thus, the researcher is assured that all authoritative pronouncements on a topic have been reviewed.

The general format of the index, which consists of four segments, is as follows:

> (1) **MAIN TERM**
> (2) Cross-references
> (3) Index strings   (4) Citations

A sample index entry which illustrates the format is presented in Figure 5-2.

The "main terms" are keywords drawn from a specially designed comprehensive list of accounting and auditing terms. Following the main term is a cross-reference listing of terms associated with the main term. Cross-references are coded BT (broader term), NT (narrower term), or RT (related term). There is a UF (used for) code which indicates synonyms for the main term and a U (use) code which indicates that the cross-reference term is used as the main term for citations in the index. The user can broaden or narrow the scope of the search by select-ing terms listed as cross-references.

Following the cross-references is a series of index strings designed to convey the subject matter of pronouncements relating to the main term. A citation for each pronouncement appears to the right of the index string. The citation is an alphanumeric code which indicates the source of the pronouncement, its number, and, if applicable, the section and paragraph number location within the reference sources.

The reader should obtain a copy of the index and become familiar with its use. There are exercises at the end of this chapter designed to provide practice on the use of the index. The reader should be aware of the "keyword" concept used as a foundation for organizing the index. The

---

Figure 5-2

ENTRY FROM *INDEX TO ACCOUNTING AND
AUDITING TECHNICAL PRONOUNCEMENTS*

AUDIT PLANNING AND SUPERVISION   *[Main term]*
  BT Auditing standards
  BT Field work standards
  BT GAAS (standards)
  BT Planning and supervision   *[Cross-references]*
  RT Analytical review procedures
  RT Audit scope

Governmental accounting Auditing
  procedures... Internal control evaluation
  Audit programs [*Index string*]   **AUG-SLG 041** *[Citation]*

Field work standards, Audit administration
  techniques, ... , Audit scope and Audit
  programs, Auditing procedures and Internal
  control evaluation [*Index string*]   **SAS 22/311** *[Citation]*

---

keywords that are used to access the index are developed in the problem
definition stage of the research process. However, the index can also be
useful in refining the statement of the problem.

AICPA Professional Standards. The *Professional Standards* series is
available in an annually updated paperback edition or in a two-volume
looseleaf subscription service as shown in Figure 5-1. The looseleaf service has the advantage of being continually updated. Volume 1 contains
the U.S. auditing standards with two major divisions: (1) Statements on
Auditing Standards (SASs) and (2) Auditing Interpretations. There are
seven topical subdivisions under Statements on Auditing Standards, as
shown in Figure 5-3. The material within each subdivision is arranged by
numbered section, and each paragraph within a section is decimally
numbered. References to sections in Volume 1 are preceded by the citation AU. To illustrate the organization and referencing system of the
Professional Standards, the table of contents of AU Section 200 is re-
produced below:

AU Section 200—**THE GENERAL STANDARDS**

Section		Paragraph
201	Nature of the General Standards	.01
210	Training and Proficiency of the Independent Auditor	.01-.05
220	Independence	.01-.07
230	Due Care in the Performance of Work	.01-.04

Figure 5-3

ORGANIZATION OF THE AICPA *PROFESSIONAL STANDARDS*

	Citation
VOLUME 1	
Statements on Auditing Standards...........................	AU Sec.
Introduction...	100
The General Standards...................................	200
The Standards of Field Work.............................	300
The First, Second, and Third Standards of Reporting	400
The Fourth Standard of Reporting	500
Special Topics..	600
Special Reports of the Committee on Auditing Procedure.....	700
Auditing Interpretations..................................	AU 9000
VOLUME 2	Citation
Accounting and Review Services	AR
Code of Professional Ethics..............................	ET
Bylaws of the AICPA.....................................	BL
International Accounting Standards	AC
International Auditing Guidelines...........................	AU*
Management Advisory Services	MS
Quality Control	QC
Tax Practice	TX

*AU 8000 series

The numbering system facilitates references to specific sections or paragraphs within a section. For example, AU Section 210.03 refers to the third paragraph of Section 210.

The second major division in Volume 1 of the *Professional Standards* is Auditing Interpretations. As discussed previously, the Interpretations provide guidance on the application of SASs. Auditing Interpretations are numbered in the 9000 series, with the last 3 digits specifying the SAS section to which an Interpretation relates. For example, AU Section 9326 indicates that the Interpretation relates to AU Section 326. Volume 1 concludes with six appendices.

Volume 2 contains eight major divisions, which are listed in Figure 5-3, along with the related citations. The material within each division is organized by numbered sections and paragraphs in the same manner as Volume 1.

A search for information on a particular subject may begin with the Master Topical Index which identifies individual indices containing detailed information. Alternatively, the researcher may go directly to the appropriate detailed index.

FASB Accounting Standards. Each year, the FASB compiles and publishes accounting standards in two complementary volumes. The first, *Original Pronouncements*, contains the complete original text of APB Opinions, Statements, and Interpretations; AICPA Accounting Research Bulletins; and FASB Statements of Concepts, Statements of Standards, Interpretations, and Technical Bulletins. The pronouncements are arranged in chronological order. All superseded and amended material is printed in a lightly colored panel to distinguish it from current material.

The other volume, *Current Text*, which is available in paperback or as a two-volume looseleaf service, is organized alphabetically by subject. The material presented under each subject begins with an integrated presentation of all pronouncements covered under Ethics Rule 203—Accounting Principles. Pronouncements not covered by Ethics Rule 203 immediately follow the official text. The reader is advised to note that the *Current Text* does not include dissenting opinions of board or committee members not in agreement with the original pronouncements. The dissenting opinions can often shed light on the scope and limitations of a pronouncement and can be located in the volume of *Original Pronouncements*.

Subjects in the *Current Text* are arranged alphabetically within two parts: (1) Part I—General Standards, which contains standards that are applicable to all entities and (2) Part III—Industry Standards, which contains standards applicable only to entities in specific industries. Part II consists of disclosure flowcharts which identify the step-by-step procedures for appropriate disclosures for particular situations.

Each section of the *Current Text* is identified by an alphanumeric code, and paragraphs within each section are decimally numbered. For example, the reference A06.110 refers to Section A06, "Accounting Changes," and paragraph 110. The *Current Text* concludes with a comprehensive Topical Index. Exercises are included at the end of this chapter which provide an opportunity to become familiar with the *Current Text*.

Technical Practice Aids. The AICPA publishes two volumes of nonauthoritative examples and commentary under the title of Technical Practice Aids (see Figure 5-1).

Volume 1 contains the Technical Information Service, which consists of a series of questions and replies. The information is categorized under major headings: Financial Statement Presentation; Assets; Liabilities and Deferred Credits; Capital; Revenue and Expense; Special Industry Problems; Special Organizational Problems; Audit Field Work; and Audit Reports.

The Technical Information Service (TIS) includes inquiries and replies based upon selected Technical Information Service correspondence dealing with various accounting or auditing issues. As a matter of policy, the TIS staff does not render opinions on tax or the legal aspects of questions submitted by practitioners. Additions to the Technical Information Service are initiated by questions from practitioners related to accounting or auditing problems. These questions are then answered by the TIS staff accountants. These responses do not represent authoritative pronouncements, but are an expression of an expert's professional opinion, supported by reference to authoritative literature if applicable. This service permits the practitioner to communicate directly with the AICPA in attempting to resolve an issue. By reading the questions and responses previously posed to the TIS, a researcher can gain insight into how other professionals have interpreted and implemented professional standards. If the particular area has not been presented to the TIS staff, the researcher can submit an inquiry. The information obtained from the TIS can be used by the researcher in forming conclusions and exercising professional judgment.

Each major section is preceded by a table of contents indicating the major topics covered. There are two appendices concluding Volume 1. The first appendix is a cross-reference index between official pronouncements cited in the volume and the section number where the pronouncement is cited. The second appendix is a keyword topical index to the volume.

Volume 2 contains the Statements of Position (SOPs) of the Accounting Standards Division and the Auditing Standards Division. These SOPs are arranged in chronological order as they are issued. The Accounting Division's SOPs are followed by a keyword topical index. Volume 2 concludes with the Quality Control Review Program.

Reading an APB Opinion or FASB Statement

In researching an issue, the researcher may be required to read a specific APB Opinion or FASB Statement. In such a case, the researcher should be aware that there is a basic format that is followed in the APB Opinions and FASB Statements. Depending upon the complexity of the pronouncement, the following elements are included: an introduction to the accounting issues addressed by the pronouncement, background of the business event and accounting issues, basis for the Board's conclusions, actual opinion or statement of accounting standard, effective date to implement the standard, illustrations of application, and disclosures required. These basic elements are not necessarily presented as separate sections of all Opinions or Statements. Those that are relatively short may combine the introduction and background information and eliminate the illustration of applications section if it is not a complicated principle. However, there is always a separate section designated as the Opinion or Standard of Accounting.

The introductory section defines the accounting issue that has necessitated an authoritative pronouncement. This section gives the scope of the pronouncement; that is, it defines the type of entity affected. It can also limit the application of the pronouncement to companies of specific size. For example, FASB Statement No. 33, "Financial Reporting and Changing Prices," is limited to public companies with inventories and fixed assets of $125 million or total assets of a billion dollars. FASB Statement No. 21, "Suspension of the Reporting of Earnings per Share and Segment Information by Non-public Enterprises," specifically limits the application of APB Opinion No. 15, "Earnings per Share," and FASB Statement No. 14, "Segment Reporting," to publicly held corporations. The introduction also gives the effects of the new pronouncement on previously issued standards. It specifies which pronouncements or sections of prior pronouncements are superseded by the new standard. Also, within the introduction there is generally a summary of the standard. Thus, the introduction quickly informs the researcher if the standard applies to the specific situation being investigated.

The background information section describes in more detail the business events and related accounting treatments presented in the pronouncement. This section develops the various arguments supporting alternative approaches to resolving the issue. The underlying assumptions for these alternatives are defined, and the different interpretations of the economic impact of the business event are presented. Within the APB Opinions, this section follows the introduction and is entitled the Discussion Section. The FASB generally places the background information in an appendix to the official pronouncement.

The basis for conclusion is described in the Opinions and Statements. This section explains the rationale for the accounting principles prescribed in the pronouncement, indicating which arguments were accepted and which were rejected. Generally, the APB incorporates the basis of conclusion within the opinion section of the pronouncement. The background information and basis for conclusion provide the researcher with a description of the business events and transactions covered by the pronouncement. These sections can be helpful in determining if the pronouncement addresses the specific issue under investigation. If the researcher is in the early stages of investigation, these sections can be helpful in defining the business transactions, determining their economic impact, and relating them to the proper reporting format.

The opinion or standard section prescribes the accounting principles that must be applied to the business transactions described in the pronouncement. The length of this section will depend upon the complexity of the business events involved.

The standard section can be very short, as in the case of FASB Statement No. 40, "Financial Reporting and Changing Prices: Specialized Assets-Timberlands and Growing Timber," which basically requires the application of FASB Statement No. 33 to timberlands. It can also be very long and complicated, as in FASB Statement No. 13, "Accounting for Leases." In Statement No. 13, the board established specialized terminology; set up criteria for distinguishing various types of leases; and established accounting, reporting, and disclosure requirements for the various leases. All of these items are within the standard section. This section represents the heart of the official pronouncement and must be followed when the researcher concludes that the standard applies to the business transactions under investigation.

The effective date section states when the new pronouncement goes into effect. It also gives any transition period which might be used by a company to implement a new standard. For example, FASB Statement No. 13 has a four-year transition period to permit companies to gather data for retroactive application of this complicated pronouncement on lease transactions. If the board prescribes the method of implementation, retroactive restatement, cumulative effect, or prospective application, the method will be indicated in this section of the pronouncement.

Summary

A major task of the researcher is that of reviewing current professional literature in the search for authoritative support. This chapter focused on the sources of authoritative support and semiauthoritative literature, as well as efficient means of accessing the literature for a solution to the issue under investigation. The resources presented include the AICPA's *Index to Accounting and Auditing Technical Pronouncements*, the AICPA's *Professional Standards* and *Technical Practice Aids*, and the *FASB Accounting Standards*. These publications provide the most comprehensive, up-to-date coverage of the current standards in every major area of professional activity plus guidance in applying the standards in practice.

In order to become more proficient with these sources, Appendices A and B to this chapter provide exercises and an illustrative problem that emphasize the methodology of the literature search step in the research process. Chapter 6 presents additional research tools with a discussion of new data bases which utilize the computer in performing the search of the professional literature. Chapter 7 attempts to refine the research process via a comprehensive problem and additional cases.

DISCUSSION QUESTIONS

1. Identify the major research tools (literature sources) that are discussed in this chapter. Also briefly describe the basic contents of each source.
2. What primary research publication would the researcher use to locate: (a) an FASB Technical Bulletin; (b) a specific Rule of Conduct in the Code

of Professional Ethics; (c) an auditing Statement of Position; (d) an Accounting Research Bulletin?

3. Explain the purpose of the "keyword" concept in accounting and/or auditing research.
4. What is the purpose of the AICPA's Technical Information Service?
5. List the major elements or segments of a specific APB Opinion or FASB Statement.

Appendix A

The following exercises emphasize the use of the *Index to Accounting and Auditing Technical Pronouncements*, the *Professional Standards*, and the *FASB Accounting Standards—Current Text*. Completion of the exercises should provide a working knowledge of these research tools. The ability to apply these tools will be tested in Chapter 7 in researching various comprehensive problems. Following the exercises are suggested solutions for self-evaluation purposes.

Exercises 1–3 relate to the use of the *Index to Accounting and Auditing Technical Pronouncements*.

1. Identify the authoritative literature indicated by the following citations:
   a. SAS 05/411
   b. ACC-SOP 75-02
   c. AUG-FCI 19
   d. SEC ASR 193
   e. ET-RLNG 591.225

2. Explain each of the following index components:
   a. COMMON STOCK EQUIVALENTS
   b. UF Residual Securities
   c. BT Securities
   d. NT Warrants (securities)
   e. RT Convertible preferred stock

3. Answer the following questions with respect to the keyword *Denial of opinion*.
   a. What main term is used for this keyword?
   b. List a broader term that could be used as a main term reference.
   c. List a narrower term that could be used as a main term reference.
   d. List some terms that are related to this keyword.

Exercises 4–6 relate to the use of the AICPA *Professional Standards*.

4. Identify the original pronouncement indicated by each of the following citations:
   a. AU Section 504
   b. AU Section 333A
   c. AU Section 9328.03–.06
   d. ET Section 301.02

5. Give citations for authoritative literature covering the following topics:
   a. Confirmation of receivables
   b. Effects of illegal acts on auditor's report
   c. Custody of audit working papers
   d. Auditor's standard report

6. Using the *Professional Standards,* locate the authoritative literature addressing the problem presented in the following situation.

   The Press-Punch Corporation is a closely held company (10 major stockholders) which manufactures parts for the three major U.S. auto companies. Two of the major stockholders formed a partnership which owns the building occupied by Press-Punch. The leasing of the building to Press-Punch is the only business activity of the partnership. As the auditor for Press-Punch you need to determine the financial statement disclosure requirements for this related party transaction.

Exercises 7 and 8 relate to the use of the FASB *Accounting Standards—Current Text*.

7. Identify the source (original pronouncement) for each of the following citations:
   a. I73.125
   b. C51.109
   c. L10.116
   d. D22.509–.513
   e. De4.108

8. The Comet Powerboat Company manufactures one of the most popular speedboats in the U.S. As an incentive to its dealers to keep an adequate stock in their showrooms, the company allows dealers to return any unsold boats at the end of the boating season.

   Locate authoritative literature in the *Current Text* which addresses the proper revenue recognition procedure for Comet Powerboat Company, taking into consideration the dealer's right to return.

Exercises 9–11 relate to the use of the FASB *Accounting Standards— Original Pronouncements.*

9. What paragraphs of the original APB Opinion No. 11 have been superseded?

10. Referring to FASB Statement No. 5, "Accounting for Contingencies," identify the paragraph numbers for the following components of the Statement.
   a. Introduction
   b. Background
   c. Basis for standard
   d. Standard of accounting and reporting
   e. Effective date
   f. Examples or illustrations

11. Referring to APB Opinion No. 26, "Early Extinguishment of Debt," identify the paragraph numbers for the following components of the Opinion.
   a. Introduction
   b. Background
   c. Basis for opinion
   d. Opinion
   e. Effective date
   f. Examples or illustrations

SOLUTIONS TO EXERCISES

	Citation	Authoritative Literature
1.	a. SAS 05/411	*Statement on Auditing Standards No. 5,* AU Section 411, "The Meaning of 'Present Fairly in Conformity with Generally Accepted Accounting Principles' in the Independent Auditor's Report."
	b. ACC-SOP 75-02	Accounting Standards Division Statement of Position 75-02, *Accounting Practices of Real Estate Investment Trusts.*
	c. AUG-FCI 19	Industry Audit Guide, *Audits of Fire and Casualty Companies,* page 19.
	d. SEC ASR 193	Securities and Exchange Commission *Accounting Series Release No. 193,* "Request by Arthur Andersen & Co. — Partial Response and Solicitation of Comments on Certain Questions."
	e. ET-RLNG 591.225	Ethics Ruling, ET Sec. 591.225, "Member's Spouse as Insurance Agent."

2. a. **COMMON STOCK EQUIVALENTS**—Main term used as the keyword reference to authoritative literature citations.

   b. **UF Residual Securities**—Indicates that the main term "common stock equivalents" is used as the keyword for "residual securities." The latter term appears in the index as a main term followed by a single cross-reference as follows:

   RESIDUAL SECURITIES
   U Common stock equivalents

   This entry directs the researcher to "use" the term *common stock equivalents* as the keyword.

   c. **BT Securities**—A term which is broader than the main term and can be used to expand the scope of the literature search. The entry under the main term "securities" includes a greater number of citations than the entry under "common stock equivalents."

   d. **NT Warrants (securities)**—A term that is narrower than the main term. Using the narrower term as a keyword or main term reduces the scope of research and therefore the number of references.

   e. **RT Convertible preferred stock**—A related term that may be used as another keyword in searching the literature.

3. a. *Disclaimers of opinion* is the main term used for *denial of opinion*.

   b. *Accountants' reports* is a broader term that could be used as a main term reference.

   c. *Piecemeal opinions* is a narrower term that could be used as a main term reference.

   d. Related terms that could be used as keywords include:
   Accountant independence
   Association with financial statements
   Audit scope limitations
   Contingencies
   Disclosures
   Unaudited financial statements

4.

Citation	Original Pronouncement
a. AU Section 504	*Statement on Auditing Standards No. 26,* "Association with Financial Statements"
b. AU Section 333A	Appendix to *Statement on Auditing Standards No. 19,* "Client Representations"
c. AU Section 9328.03–.06	Auditing Interpretation, "Material Weaknesses in Accounting Control and the Foreign Corrupt Practices Act" (Interpretation No. 2 of SAS No. 17, "Illegal Acts by Clients")

d. ET Section 301.02   Ethics Interpretation 301-1, "Confidential Information and Technical Standards" (Interpretation under Rule 301, "Confidential Client Information")

5.

Topic	Citations
a. Confirmation of receivables	AU Sections 327.12; 331.01–.08; 9509.01
b. Effects of illegal acts on auditor's report	AU Sections 328.14–.17
c. Custody of audit working papers	AU Sections 339.06–.08
d. Auditor's standard report	AU Sections 509.06–.08; 509.30

6. Some keywords that could be used to locate relevant authoritative literature are:

> Closely Held Companies
> Disclosure
> Leases
> Related Parties

Statement on Auditing Standards No. 6, "Related Party Transactions," sets forth the disclosure requirements for transactions involving related parties. SAS No. 6 is located in the *Professional Standards* at AU Section 335. The disclosure requirements are specified in Sections 335.16–.18. Interpretations relating to related party disclosures are located in Sections 9335.01–.09.

The relevant citations can be located in the AU Topical Index under "Related Parties—Disclosure Requirements" or "Disclosure—Related Party Transactions." There are no relevant citations under the other keywords listed.

7.

Citation	Source (Pronouncement)
a. I73.125	APB Opinion No. 28, par. 22
b. C51.109	Accounting Research Bulletin No. 51, par. 6
c. L10.116	FASB Statement of Financial Accounting Standards No. 13, par. 20
d. D22.509–.513	FASB Technical Bulletin 81-6
e. De4.108	FASB Interpretation No. 7. par. 12

8. Some keywords that could be used in the literature search are:

> Revenue Recognition
> Sales Returns
> Right of Return

"Revenue Recognition" is the appropriate keyword in this case. A reference to Section R75.105–.109 is found in the *Current Text* Topical

Index under "Revenue Recognition—Right of Return." The source for this section is FASB Statement No. 48, "Revenue Recognition When Right of Return Exists."

9. Paragraphs 38, 39, 40, and 41 of APB Opinion No. 11 have been superseded.

10. FASB Statement No. 5:   Paragraphs
    a. Introduction   1-7
    b. Background   46-54
    c. Basis for standard   55-104
    d. Standard of accounting and reporting   8-19
    e. Effective date   20
    f. Examples or illustrations..........................   21-45

11. APB Opinion No. 26:   Paragraphs
    a. Introduction   1-3
    b. Background   4-17
    c. Basis for opinion   20
    d. Opinion..   18-21
    e. Effective date   22
    f. Examples or illustrations..........................   None

Appendix B

ILLUSTRATIVE PROBLEM

The Johnson Furniture Company, an audit client, is a furniture dealer in Havan, South Carolina. Johnson sells a fine line of quality constructed furniture with sales ranging from small accessories to complete rooms of furniture. Financing options available to customers include: (1) cash payments within 30 days with no interest charge or (2) installment sales with a periodic rate of 1.5 percent per month, which is an annual rate of 18 percent.

In need of cash, Johnson's management recently decided to sell $170,000 of accounts receivable to Security Finance Company. The finance company paid Johnson $174,600 for those receivables. The differential of $4,600 was recorded in Johnson's books as revenue from the sale of receivables. The facts concerning the receivables sold are as follows.

Net receivables	$170,000
Add finance charges (18% annual effective rate of interest) ...	51,000
Total amount of installments..............................	$221,000

Amount for which receivables are sold (total amount
   of installments discounted to yield 16% to the buyer) $174,600
Net receivables   170,000
Differential... $ 4,600

The receivables were purchased by Security on a recourse basis. The Johnson Furniture Company has agreed to be responsible for the collection of the receivables. If a customer defaults on payment, Johnson agrees to pay the remainder of that customer's balance and to be responsible for repossession of the merchandise.

As the auditor for Johnson Furniture Company, you question the recognition of the differential as revenue for the current period. The client requests authoritative support for any other treatment of the $4,600.

SUGGESTED SOLUTION

Step 1—Problem Identification. The Johnson Furniture Company has sold receivables on a recourse basis resulting in a positive differential. How should this differential be accounted for?

Analysis of the transaction indicates that income may be overstated on the income statement, and liabilities may be understated on the balance sheet. Following is a refined statement of the problem:

> When accounts receivable are sold on a recourse basis, what is the proper method for recognizing revenue arising from a positive differential?

Step 2—Evidence Collection. From the problem statement, the following keywords can be identified and used to access the professional literature:

> Accounts Receivable
> Sales
> Installment Receivables
> Revenue Recognition

Using these keywords, citations are located in the *Index to Accounting and Auditing Technical Pronouncements* as follows:

Keyword	Citation
Accounts Receivable	
(BT) Receivables	ACC-SOP 74-06
Sales......................................	ACC-SOP 74-06
Installment Receivables	
(BT) Receivables	ACC-SOP 74-06
Revenue Recognition......................	ACC-SOP 74-06

There were no relevant citations under the keywords "Accounts Receivable" or "Installment Receivables." Each of these terms referenced a broader term (BT) "Receivables." Under the broader term was an index string entitled "Revenue recognition for Sales of . . . with recourse" with the citation ACC-SOP 74-06. Two of the other keywords also provide an index string with reference to the same citation.

ACC-SOP 74-06 refers to a Statement of Position of the Accounting Standards Division of the AICPA. This pronouncement is located in the *Technical Practice Aids* loose-leaf service.

The researcher may also wish to review issues of *Accounting Trends & Techniques* (discussed in Chapter 6) for possible clues to how others have handled similar situations.

Step 3—Evaluation of Results. Upon reviewing the Statement of Position 74-06, the following facts were discovered.

The Accounting Standards Division of the AICPA reviewed the area of sales of receivables with recourse and found that two methods of revenue recognition were being used: (1) the delayed recognition method and (2) the immediate recognition method.

Under the delayed recognition method, the differential is recognized as income over a period of time—the installment period. The reasons for using the delayed recognition method were as follows:

a) A sale of receivables with recourse is in substance a type of financing, in effect a borrowing by the seller.

b) If the receivable had been kept rather than being sold, the owner would have collected interest over the installment period and recognized interest income. The differential is similar to interest.

c) Realization occurs with the passage of time as the risks retained by the seller are diminished over time by the installment payments.

d) As the receivables are paid, the risk of default diminishes and therefore a corresponding amount of the differential can be recognized.

The immediate recognition method considers the sale of receivables with recourse a completed transaction, therefore the profit or loss is recognized immediately.

Regarding the application of generally accepted accounting principles to the sale of receivables with recourse, the Division referenced revenue recognition in APB Statement No. 4, paragraphs 148-153. Realization is described as follows: "Revenue is generally recognized when both of the following conditions are met: (1) the earning process is complete or virtually complete, and (2) an exchange has taken place" (paragraph 150). Also, APB Statement No. 4 holds that the realization principle requires that revenue be earned before it is recognized as income, and revenue from permitting others to use a business's resources (such as interest, rent, and royalties) is recognized as time passes or as the resources are used.

The Accounting Standards Division reviewed the two primary methods of accounting for profits or losses on the sale of receivables with recourse. Based upon their views, the Division recommends the use of the delayed method because of the risk of default on the payment of the receivable.

Step 4 — Conclusion and Documentation. Based upon ACC-SOP 74-06, the conclusion is that Johnson Furniture Company should use the delayed method. The following research memo should be prepared for complete documentation of the accounting problem.

Research Memorandum

Regarding Johnson Furniture Company
From: Audit Supervisor

Johnson Furniture Company, an audit client, sells furniture to customers on either the cash basis or the installment basis. In need of additional cash, Johnson sold accounts receivable to Security Finance Company on a recourse basis. During the audit of accounts receivable, it was discovered that Johnson used the immediate recognition method for the positive differential resulting from the sale of the receivables to the finance company. An investigation of authoritative literature was conducted to determine the acceptability of this method.

The specific problem researched was stated as follows: When accounts receivable are sold on a recourse basis, what is the proper method for recognizing revenue arising from a positive differential?

The literature search produced one primary reference, Statement of Position 74-06 of the Accounting Standards Division of the AICPA. Based upon the Statement of Position, the preferred method for recognizing revenue from the differential is the delayed method, whereby the differential is amortized over the period of the installment sale. This method is recommended because of the risk of default on the payment of the receivable.

OTHER RESEARCH TOOLS

The previous chapters have presented a practical approach to conducting accounting and auditing research. Chapter 5 dealt with the search for authoritative support through the use of traditional manual research tools — the FASB's *Accounting Standards* and the AICPA's *Index to Accounting and Auditing Technical Pronouncements*, *Professional Standards*, and *Technical Practice Aids*.

This chapter focuses on other manual research tools and on computerized research tools currently available. Due to the increase in accounting and auditing pronouncements and the increase in financial reporting in general, more and more organizations are utilizing computerized research tools to gain rapid access to key information for decision making.

Manual Research Tools

In addition to those discussed in Chapter 5, other frequently used manual research tools include the AICPA's *Accountants' Index, Accounting*

Trends & Techniques, Financial Report Surveys, and *Audit and Accounting Manual;* Leasco Systems and Research Corporation's microfiche service; research files of public accounting firms; and public files of the accounting and auditing authoritative bodies.

Accountants' Index. The *Accountants' Index* is a comprehensive subject/author index published by the AICPA. Since this publication is the index to the AICPA's library, all materials are available on a loan basis to members of the Institute. The index, which is arranged in a dictionary format with full citations, covers virtually every English-language publication on accounting or accounting-related subjects, such as data processing, financial management, investments and securities, management, and taxation. The index, published in quarterly and yearly supplements, provides quick access to a number of books, articles, pamphlets, speeches, and government documents. Figure 6-1 presents an excerpt from the index.

Figure 6–1

EXCERPT FROM *ACCOUNTANTS' INDEX*

ACCOUNTANTS' INDEX 1981   Byrd, Kerry.

BUY-AND-SELL AGREEMENTS
  See Purchase agreements
    Taxation, United States — Purchase
    agreements

BUYING AND SELLING A BUSINESS
  See also Taxation, United States —
    Purchases and sales
  Asset redeployment: everything is for sale
    now. (Corporate finance) *Business week,*
    Aug. 24, 1981, p. 68-72, 74.
  Chazen, Leonard. Fairness from a financial
    point of view in acquisitions of public
    companies; is third-party sale value the
    appropriate standard? *Business lawyer,*
    v. 36, July 1981, p. 1439-81.
  Riebold, Mary A. So you think you acquired
    a pension clean slate? (An open letter
    from a seller to a buyer). *Journal of pension
    planning and compliance,* v. 4, July 1981,
    p. 261-72.

BUYOUTS
  Corncel, Frederic G. Dealing with con-
    flicts in family corporations. (In Institute
    On Estate Planning, 15th, University of
    Miami Law Center, 1981. *Proceedings,*
    New York, c1981. p. 18-1 - 18-34. [750.2]

Lewis, David L. Planning for short-term
  needs of surviving spouse. (In Institute
  On Federal Taxation, 39th, New York
  University, 1980. *Proceedings.* New York,
  c1981. v. 2, pp. 44-1 - 44-11.) [751 N]

BUYS, DONNA
  Nursing management must be strength-
    ened, *Modern health-care,* v. 11, Aug.
    1981, p. 100, 102.

BUZBY, STEPHEN L.
  Discussion of: DAAM: the demand for al-
    ternative accounting measurements, by
    Stephen L. Buzby and Haim Falk. (In Con-
    ference On Research In Accounting, 13th,
    University of Chicago, 1978. *Studies on
    accounting for changes in general and specific
    prices; empirical research and public policy
    issues.* Chicago, 1979. p. 37-45.) [*102C]

BYLER, ROBERT.
  Teaching college students association com-
    munications. *Association management,* v. 33,
    July 1981, p. 72-5.

BYRD, KERRY.
  Polk, Warren J. Managing the very large
    database, by Warren J. Polk and Kerry
    Byrd. *Datamation,* v. 27, Sept. 1981,
    p. 114-16, 118, 120, 122, 124.

Accounting Trends & Techniques. *Accounting Trends & Techniques* is an annual publication of the AICPA which illustrates the current reporting practices of a selected group of companies and charts significant trends in reporting practices. The companies surveyed are all publicly held, and 90 percent of them are listed on the New York or American Stock Exchanges.

The survey enables the practitioner to determine how companies of various sizes in a wide range of industries have complied with the professional standards as they relate to financial reporting. It also alerts the practitioner to emerging trends in reporting practices. Specific reporting requirements set forth in pronouncements of the APB, FASB, and SEC are cited wherever applicable.

Each company surveyed in *Accounting Trends & Techniques* is assigned a reference number. As companies are removed from the survey because of acquisition or merger, the identification number is retired. There is an appendix listing the companies in the order of their reference numbers. The survey contains a table of contents listing specific reporting and disclosure examples by the general categories of Balance Sheet, Income Statement, Stockholders Equity, Statement of Changes in Financial Position, and Auditor's Report. A topical index is included at the end of the survey. An excerpt from *Accounting Trends & Techniques* is presented in Figure 6-2.

Financial Report Surveys. The AICPA's *Financial Report Surveys* are a continuing series of studies designed to show in detail how specific accounting and reporting questions are actually being handled in the financial reports of companies in a wide range of industries. The surveys include numerous illustrations drawn from the National Automated Accounting Research System (NAARS), which stores data collected from thousands of published financial reports. They also include the complete texts of official pronouncements and other pertinent material wherever applicable. To date, the AICPA has published the following surveys, each focusing in depth on a specific issue of financial reporting:

1. *Accounting Policy Disclosure.* Application of APB Opinion No. 22. (1972)
2. *Reporting Accounting Changes.* Reporting under APB Opinion No. 20. (1974)
3. *Reporting Results of Operations.* Reporting under APB Opinion No. 30. (1974)
4. *Interperiod Tax Allocation.* Application of APB Opinion Nos. 11, 23, 24, and 25 and SEC Release No. 149. (1974)
5. *Statement of Changes in Financial Position.* Reporting under APB Opinion No. 19. (1974)
6. *Summary of Operations and Related Management Discussion and Analysis.* Application of Rules 14a-3 and 14c-3 of the Securities Exchange Act of 1934 in annual reports to shareholders. (1975)

Figure 6-2

EXCERPT FROM *ACCOUNTING TRENDS & TECHNIQUES*

conditions, if the purchase price of the aggregate minority interest were computed in accordance with the agreements as of December 27, 1980, such purchase price would exceed the recorded amount of such minority interest by approximately $11,200,000. The Company is substituted for the subsidiary, if the subsidiary fails to make such purchase.

MOSINEE PAPER CORPORATION (DEC)

NOTES TO CONSOLIDATED FINANCIAL STATEMENTS

Note 10 (in part): Commitments, Contingencies, Litigation, and Related Party Transactions

The Company has an agreement with two executives and officers which commits the Company to repurchase 50,000 shares of common stock at the prevailing market price less $6.25 per share. The repurchase commitment, if requested on December 31, 1980, would have amounted to $56,250.

SUPREME EQUIPMENT & SYSTEM CORP. (JUL)

NOTES TO THE CONSOLIDATED FINANCIAL STATEMENTS

Note 10 (in part): Commitments and Contingencies:

B) The company and its principal stockholder have entered into an agreement which contains a provision that the company, upon demand, will repurchase certain of his shares in the event of his death. The purchase price will be based on the market value of the company's shares during a specified period prior to the repurchase date, but is limited to $500,000. The company has sufficient insurance on the life of the principal stockholder to meet its obligation under this agreement.

Completion Agreement

ALUMINUM COMPANY OF AMERICA (DEC)

NOTES TO FINANCIAL STATEMENTS

(In millions, except share amounts)

Note H: Commitments and Contingent Liabilities

Guarantees on outstanding indebtedness of others totaled $83.7 at December 31, 1980, including $58.6 applicable to an affiliate which operates a bauxite mining project in the Republic of Guinea.

In December 1980 Alcoa Aluminio S.A., a Brazilian subsidiary, signed a Credit Agreement with an international syndicate of banks providing for borrowings of up to $750 to finance its expansion program. This program involves primarily the construction of a large alumina refining and aluminum smelting complex at Sao Luis in the State of Maranhao, Brazil. Prior to any drawdown under the Credit Agreement Alcoa must enter into a Completion Agreement under which it will agree (1) to use its best efforts to cause that complex to be completed by Alcoa Aluminio and (2) to cause Alcoa Aluminio to obtain funds or to provide funds to Alcoa Aluminio sufficient to ensure Alcoa Aluminio's compliance with certain financial covenants set forth in that Credit Agreement. These obligations of Alcoa would continue until certain tests of completion are satisfied or until Alcoa's performance is excused by the occurrence and continuance of any specified event of

sovereign relief such as expropriation or insurrection and until the financial covenants referred to above are complied with.

SUBSEQUENT EVENTS

Events or transactions which occur subsequent to the balance sheet date but prior to the issuance of the financial statements and which have a material effect on the financial statements should be either reflected or disclosed in the statements. Section 560 of *Statement on Auditing Standards No. 1* sets forth criteria for the proper treatment of subsequent events.

Table 1-12 classifies disclosures of subsequent events included in the 1980 annual reports on the survey companies.

Examples of subsequent event disclosures follow.

Business Combinations

AMF INCORPORATED (DEC)

NOTES TO CONSOLIDATED FINANCIAL STATEMENTS

Note 1 (in part): Acquisitions

On February 6, 1981, the Company also acquired the stock of Scientific Drilling International (SDI) for two million shares of AMF common stock. SDI is a privately owned Irvine, California based company which provides worldwide orientation and survey equipment and related services to the oil field directional drilling market. The acquisition will be accounted for as a pooling of interests. On a combined pro-forma basis, AMF's revenue, net income, and earnings per share would have been as follows (in thousands of dollars):

	1980	1979	1978
Revenue	$1,563,330	$1,457,344	$1,330,444
Net Income	$ 58,506	$ 54,159	$ 46,354
EPS	$2.60	$2.43	$2.09

TABLE 1-12: SUBSEQUENT EVENTS

	Number of Companies			
	1980	1979	1978	1977
Business combinations pending or effected	36	51	62	51
Debt incurred, reduced or refinanced	22	29	17	33
Stock splits or dividends	20	12	16	7
Sale of assets	19	19	19	14
Litigation	10	11	7	19
Other—described	38	33	39	19

7. *Departures from the Auditor's Standard Report.* Application of SAS No. 2. (1975)
8. *Disclosure of Related Party Transactions.* (1975)
9. *Disclosure of Subsequent Events.* Application of Section 560 of SAS No. 1. (1976)
10. *Accounting for Contingencies.* Application of FASB Statement Nos. 5 and 11. (1976)
11. *Disclosure of Pro Forma Calculations.* Application of APB Opinion Nos. 15, 16, and 20 and SAS No. 1. (1976)
12. *Accounting for Marketable Equity Securities.* Application of FASB Statement No. 12. (1977)
13. *Disclosure of Unaudited Financial Information in Audited Financial Statements.* (1977)
14. *Accounting for Employee Benefits.* (1977)
15. *Updated Accounting Policy Disclosure.* Application of APB Opinion No. 22. (1978)
16. *Accounting for Leases.* Application of FASB Statement No. 13. (1978)
17. *Accounting for Debt Under Four Pronouncements.* Application of APB Opinion No. 26 and FASB Statement Nos. 4, 6, and 15. (1978)
18. *Illustrations of Auditors' Reports on Comparative Financial Statements.* Application of SAS No. 15. (1979)
19. *Management Reports on Financial Statements.* Application of the conclusions and recommendations of the AICPA Special Advisory Committee on Reports by Management. (1979)
20. *Illustrations of Selected Proxy Information.* Application of SEC requirements to disclose auditors' services and management perquisites in proxy statements. (1979)
21. *Accounting for Joint Ventures.* Application of various methods of accounting for joint ventures in the financial statements. (1980)
22. *Disclosures of Pension Information.* Illustrations and analyses of disclosure requirements of FASB Statement No. 36. (1981)
23. *Disclosures of Inflation Accounting Information.* Application of the requirements of FASB Statement Nos. 33, 39, 40, and 41. (1982)
24. *Foreign Currency Translation.* Application of the provisions of FASB Statement No. 52. (1982)

Audit and Accounting Manual. The *Audit and Accounting Manual,* prepared by the staff of the AICPA, provides a nonauthoritative guide for practitioners in the conduct of an audit. The manual explains and illustrates the actual procedures involved in major aspects of an audit engagement. Extensive examples of such items as engagement letters, audit programs, working papers, and various other forms and documents are provided. The contents of the manual include the following:

- Engagement Planning and Administration
- Internal Control

- Audit Approach and Programs
- Working Papers
- Correspondence, Confirmations, and Representations
- Disclosure Checklists
- Review and Report Processing
- Accountants' Reports
- Financial Statements

Examples and exhibits in the manual are presented for illustrative purposes only. Many sections, however, provide references to authoritative pronouncements in the AICPA *Professional Standards*. The *Audit and Accounting Manual* is available in an annual paperback edition or as a looseleaf subscription service.

Microfiche Service. Leasco Systems and Research Corporation provides a service that includes the following information on microfiche:

1. Annual reports to shareholders for all companies filing with the SEC.
2. Forms 8-K and 10-K reports filed with the SEC.
3. Proxies, registration statements, and prospectuses filed with the SEC.

One 4 × 6-inch microfiche can store up to 60 pages of information and aids in reviewing how various firms report information to the SEC.

Research Files of Public Accounting Firms. Many public accounting firms maintain a research file on various accounting and auditing issues documented from the firm's own practice. The primary purpose of such a file is to provide firm personnel with access to previously researched issues and the firm's conclusions. The research file's design can be as simple or advanced as necessary to meet the firm's needs.

When confronted with a research issue, the practitioner searches the file index to determine if the issue has been researched and, if so, where the details of the research can be located. The index is typically an alphanumeric listing by subject matter of topics which are stored in the research files. The details of the research (e.g., research memorandums discussed in Chapter 4) may be stored on microfilm or microfiche to reduce storage costs.

APB, FASB, AccSEC, and ASB Files. The public files of the APB, FASB, AccSEC, and the ASB contain useful information for the researcher. The public files include all exposure drafts, letters of comment in response to the drafts, minutes of meetings, agenda items, and other correspondence related to the development of professional standards and other pronouncements, such as interpretations. The information contained in these files provides valuable insight in determining the rationale of the various boards or committees in developing standards.

Professional Library. Every accounting firm should establish and periodically update a professional library for research purposes. The research publications discussed in Chapter 5 and in preceding sections of this chapter represent the most comprehensive sources of authoritative and nonauthoritative accounting and auditing literature. There are many other reference sources which can aid the practitioner in conducting accounting and auditing research. It is not possible to list every publication in the area of accounting, auditing, and related topics. However, the AICPA prepares a suggested list of publications to serve as a guide in establishing a professional library.[1] The list is divided into two major sections: (1) a basic reference library and (2) supplements to the basic library.

Publications suggested for the *basic reference library* include the following:

1. Official Pronouncements and Interpretations of AICPA Senior and Technical Committees—
   - *Professional Standards*
   - *Industry Accounting and Audit Guides*
2. FASB *Financial Accounting Standards*
3. SEC Accounting Releases (ASRs, FFRs, and AAERs) and Regulation S-X
4. General References—A list of nonauthoritative reference books, primarily handbooks, manuals, and guides.
5. Tax Services—A partial list of available tax services. (The AICPA recommends at least one federal income tax loose-leaf service for a basic library and additional services depending on the firm's needs.)
6. AICPA Publications
   - *Accountants' Index.*
   - *Accounting Trends & Techniques.*
   - *Audit and Accounting Manual.*
   - *An Auditor's Approach to Statistical Sampling.* Volumes 1, 2, 3, 5, and 6.
   - *Auditor's Study and Evaluation of Internal Control in EDP Systems.*
   - Carmichael, Douglas R. *The Auditor's Reporting Obligation.* 1972.
   - Carmichael, Douglas R. *Corporate Financial Reporting.* 1976.
   - Davis, Gordon B. *Auditing & EDP.* 1968.
   - *Financial Report Surveys.*
   - *GAAP for Smaller and/or Closely Held Businesses.*
   - *Index to Accounting and Auditing Technical Pronouncements.*

---

[1]AICPA, *Management of an Accounting Practice Handbook* (New York: AICPA, 1981), Vol. 3, Chap. 505.

- *Management Advisory Services by CPAs.*
- Management Advisory Services Guidelines Series.
- *Management of an Accounting Practice Handbook.*
- *Report, Conclusions and Recommendations — Final Report of the Commission on Auditors' Responsibilities.*
- Roberts, Donald. *Statistical Auditing.* 1978.
- Statements of Position of the Accounting Standards Divison.
- Statements on Standards for Accounting and Review Services.
- *Technical Practice Aids.*
7. Periodicals and Newsletters —
   - *Accounting Review.* Sarasota, Fla.: American Accounting Association.
   - *AICPA Washington Report.* New York: American Institute of Certified Public Accountants.
   - *CPA Letter.* New York: American Institute of Certified Public Accountants.
   - *Journal of Accountancy.* New York: American Institute of Certified Public Accountants.
   - *Journal of Taxation.* Boston: Warren, Gorham & Lamont.
   - *Management Accounting.* New York: National Association of Accountants.
   - *Practical Accountant.* New York: Institute for Continuing Professional Development.
   - *Practicing CPA.* New York: American Institute of Certified Public Accountants.
   - *Tax Adviser.* New York: American Institute of Certified Public Accountants.
   - *Taxation for Accountants.* Boston: Warren, Gorham & Lamont.

Supplements to the basic library include a list of publications from which selections can be made according to the firm's needs. Supplementary publications are listed under the following topics:

1. Accounting Theory, Principles, and Practices
2. Cost and Managerial Accounting
3. Governmental Accounting
4. Specialized Accounting Systems and Practice
5. Statement Analysis and Interpretation
6. Auditing
7. Internal and Operational Auditing
8. Taxation
9. Budgeting
10. Commercial Law
11. Investment and Security Analysis
12. Mathematics of Finance
13. Organization and Management
14. Small Business

Computerized Research Tools

Computerized research tools consist of various data bases that are available which provide information compiled from a number of sources. The researcher utilizes the computer to access the data base to retrieve relevant information. The National Automated Accounting Research System is the most comprehensive data base for conducting accounting and auditing research. Other data bases which may be of use to the researcher are briefly described.

National Automated Accounting Research System. *NAARS,* an acronym for National Automated Accounting Research System, is a computerized information retrieval system developed by the AICPA and Mead Data Central, Inc. (MDC). Through the use of a terminal which is linked to MDC's computer system, a researcher is able to access the financial statements, footnotes, and auditors' reports from the published annual reports of over 8,000 companies and also the current text of authoritative and nonauthoritative literature. Presently, the NAARS library consists of the following active files:

1. *Annual Report File* — Annual reports to shareholders of corporations whose stock is traded on the New York or American Stock Exchanges or over-the-counter; includes financial statements, footnotes, auditor's report, and management responsibility letter.
2. *Management Discussion and Analysis File* — Management's discussion and analysis of operations contained in the annual report.
3. *Proxy File* — Selected elements contained in proxy statements.
4. *Accounting Literature File* — The full updated text of all currently effective pronouncements that relate to financial reporting.
5. *Archive File* — Annual report files commencing with 1972-73.

NAARS has four characteristics which make it a unique retrieval system. First, it is a "full text" system because every word of every document on file is recorded in a data base. Each word of the text is treated as an index term. Therefore, the researcher can retrieve a document based upon the words in the document. The research display could include the full text of the document, a specific segment, or a search word surrounded by a small amount of the text in order to determine the context of the search word.

Secondly, NAARS is a real time system whereby the researcher using a terminal can communicate directly with the data base via telephone lines from the researcher's office. Thirdly, the system operates in an interactive mode which permits the researcher to carry on a dialogue with the computer. Thus the researcher can broaden or narrow the search by modifying the information retrieved. Finally, NAARS has multiple-term coordinate search capabilities. This characteristic allows the researcher to create strings of words or phrases to be searched by the system.

Although NAARS is only one of many research tools available, it has many advantages in terms of speed of research, the versatility to expand or narrow the focus of research, and a relatively low cost.

Other Data Bases. Various data bases are available which cover a wide variety of subjects. Those that are most likely to be of use to the accountant or auditor are described in the following sections.

LEXIS, NEXIS, and DISCLO. In addition to NAARS, three other data bases are available through Mead Data Central. LEXIS is a legal data base which contains federal law libraries, state law libraries of all 50 states, and the United Kingdom law libraries. Also included in the LEXIS data base are Auto-Cite, which verifies case-law citations, and the Encyclopedia Britannica. NEXIS provides access to recent news articles from various major newspapers, magazines, and wire services. DISCLO is prepared by Disclosure, Inc., and is included in Mead Data Central's data bases. This data base includes excerpts from 10-K and 20-F filings, proxy statements, and initial registration statements filed with the SEC by public companies.

DIALOG and ORBIT. DIALOG, prepared by DIALOG Information Services, Inc., and ORBIT, prepared by SDC Search Service, are data bases that extract information on a variety of subjects. The data bases include such topics as agriculture, energy, business, economics, governmental publications, chemistry, law, medicine, science, and engineering.

Value Line. The FASB, in conjunction with various accounting firms and universities, has developed a data base on changing prices information. This computerized data base, which is accessible through Value Line, provides valuable information from different projects that have focused on and analyzed FASB Statement No. 33 — "Financial Reporting and Changing Prices."

Standard & Poor's News Service. This computerized data bank contains information from Standard & Poor's *Corporation Records*, *Current News Editions*, and the *Daily News Edition*. Up-to-date information in this data base includes interim earnings, dividends, contract awards, management changes, bond descriptions, and mergers.

New York Times Information Bank. This information bank, prepared by the New York Times Company, contains abstracts from some 55 journals which cover all aspects of business, economics, and political topics.

Dow Jones Retrieval Service. The Dow Jones Retrieval Service, prepared by Dow Jones and Company, consists of a data base containing current news items from the *Wall Street Journal, Barron's,* and the *Dow Jones News Service.* Also included are market quotations, earnings estimates, and industry and statistical data.

Summary

Many research tools are available to the accountant/auditor in conducting practical research. The major tools can be classified as either manual or computerized retrieval systems. As business information in general expands, computerized data bases will no doubt become the primary research tools in the future.

DISCUSSION QUESTIONS

1. Describe the contents of the following manual research tools: *Accountants' Index, Accounting Trends & Techniques, Financial Report Surveys, Audit and Accounting Manual.*
2. What is the purpose of a public accounting firm's research file?
3. Identify the four major characteristics of NAARS.
4. List some advantages of computerized research over manual research.
5. Describe the contents of the following data bases: LEXIS, DISCLO, and Dow Jones Retrieval Service.

Chapter 7

REFINING THE RESEARCH PROCESS

The preceding chapters have laid the foundation for conducting efficient and effective applied accounting and auditing research. At this point in the text, the reader should be somewhat familiar with the various manual and computerized research tools and should have a clear understanding of the basic four-step research process.

This chapter presents a comprehensive problem which illustrates the research process in detail. Specific steps and procedures for conducting and documenting the research process are summarized in Figure 7-1, which presents a flowchart depicting an overview of the complete research process. Each step should be executed and documented for every research project.

Following this chapter are two case studies (Appendix A) which provide an opportunity for testing and further developing research skills by applying the techniques presented in this text. Appendix B provides suggested solutions to the case studies.

Figure 7-1

OVERVIEW OF THE RESEARCH PROCESS

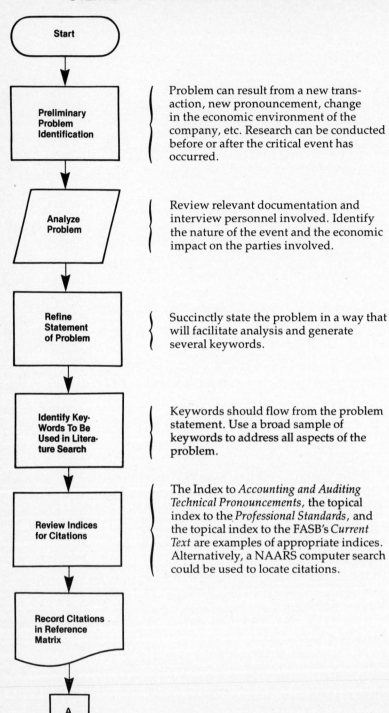

Start

Preliminary Problem Identification

Problem can result from a new trans-action, new pronouncement, change in the economic environment of the company, etc. Research can be conducted before or after the critical event has occurred.

Analyze Problem

Review relevant documentation and interview personnel involved. Identify the nature of the event and the economic impact on the parties involved.

Refine Statement of Problem

Succinctly state the problem in a way that will facilitate analysis and generate several keywords.

Identify Key-Words To Be Used in Litera-ture Search

Keywords should flow from the problem statement. Use a broad sample of keywords to address all aspects of the problem.

Review Indices for Citations

The Index to *Accounting and Auditing Technical Pronouncements,* the topical index to the *Professional Standards,* and the topical index to the FASB's *Current Text* are examples of appropriate indices. Alternatively, a NAARS computer search could be used to locate citations.

Record Citations in Reference Matrix

A

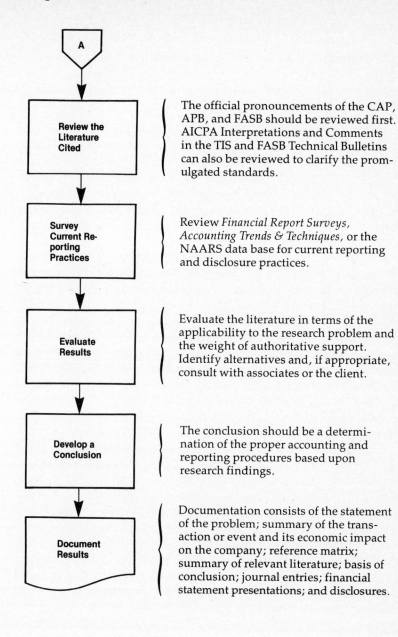

Review the Literature Cited

The official pronouncements of the CAP, APB, and FASB should be reviewed first. AICPA Interpretations and Comments in the TIS and FASB Technical Bulletins can also be reviewed to clarify the promulgated standards.

Survey Current Reporting Practices

Review *Financial Report Surveys, Accounting Trends & Techniques,* or the NAARS data base for current reporting and disclosure practices.

Evaluate Results

Evaluate the literature in terms of the applicability to the research problem and the weight of authoritative support. Identify alternatives and, if appropriate, consult with associates or the client.

Develop a Conclusion

The conclusion should be a determination of the proper accounting and reporting procedures based upon research findings.

Document Results

Documentation consists of the statement of the problem; summary of the transaction or event and its economic impact on the company; reference matrix; summary of relevant literature; basis of conclusion; journal entries; financial statement presentations; and disclosures.

Comprehensive Problem

The following is an illustrative problem that is used to demonstrate the application of the research methodology depicted in Figure 7-1. The problem should be followed carefully in order to comprehend the complete research process.

Keller Realty Inc. is a national real estate firm. The firm was incorporated in 1976, and Alex Keller, the founder and president, is the majority stockholder. During the late 1970's, Keller decided to expand his successful regional real estate firm into a national operation. He established offices in major cities across the country. The corporation leased all of the office space. The standard lease agreement included a 10-year, noncancellable term and a 5-year option renewable at the discretion of the lessee.

During the years 1980-82, the residential home market became severely depressed due to tight monetary policies and high interest rates. Because of the depressed market, Keller decided to retrench and reduce the scope of the company's operations. At that time the company had 75 offices around the country, and Keller decided to eliminate 25 offices located in depressed economic areas which Keller believed would not experience a recovery in the housing market in the succeeding five years. During 1982, Keller Realty Inc. did close the 25 offices. The realty company, however, was bound by the lease agreements on these office buildings. The company was able to sublease 10 of the buildings but continued to make lease payments on 15 vacated offices.

The lease commitments have been properly classified as operating leases. The controller for the company, Elaine Wise, has expressed concern to Keller about the proper accounting for the lease commitments on the 15 offices that have not been subleased. Wise feels that the future lease commitments should be recognized as a loss for the current period. Keller disagrees, however, and believes that the rental payments are period costs which should be recognized as expense in the year paid. Keller is confident that the vacant offices can be subleased within the next year, and there is no need to book a loss and corresponding liability in this accounting period. He has, however, given the controller the task of researching this problem and making a recommendation supported by current authoritative pronouncements.

Problem Identification, Analysis, and Refinement. The initial step in the research process is identification of a potential problem. In this situation the controller has recognized a potential problem in the accounting and reporting treatment of lease commitments on vacated buildings. It should be noted that the president, Alex Keller, does not agree that a problem exists. He believes that the fact that the buildings are vacant does not change the nature of the lease commitment, and there is no need for changing the established accounting and reporting procedures. It is the problem recognition by the controller that initiates the entire research process.

The initial statement of the problem could be written as follows: "Should a loss be recognized in the current period from lease commitments on vacant offices?" The controller examines the lease agreements and finds the following information:

1. The lease agreements were prepared by Karen Roth, attorney for Keller Realty Inc. All the leases were standardized, and the details were filled in for specific locations.
2. The terms of the lease require the lessee to make all the monthly payments over the noncancellable term of the lease or find a sublessee suitable to the lessor.
3. A summary of the lease commitments was prepared by the controller as follows:

Number of Leases	Monthly Rental Rate	Noncancellable Terms in Months	Total Commitment
10	$1,500	60	$900,000
5	2,500	60	750,000

4. In discussing the lease agreements with the lawyer, the controller learned that Keller Realty Inc. is bound by the terms of the leases and would probably be sued by the lessors and forced to make the lease payments if the company dishonored its commitment.
5. Ken Riley, the general manager at the company headquarters, is responsible for subleasing the vacated offices. He indicated in a discussion with the controller that it is highly unlikely that all of the vacant offices would be subleased. He explained that the 10 offices which had been subleased were in areas that were not severely depressed. The remaining 15 offices will be more difficult to sublease. He feels confident that he can sublease 5 offices by the middle of the next fiscal year, but doubts that the remaining properties can be subleased. At worst, none of the 15 vacated properties would be subleased. Under the terms of existing subleases, the monthly rent paid by the sublessees equals the rent expense which the realty company was obligated to pay under the original leases. Riley indicated that each of the 5 additional offices which he expects to sublease can be rented for $1,500 per month, the amount currently paid by the realty company.
6. The company's incremental borrowing rate is currently 16%.

After considering the information gathered through a review of the lease documents and discussions with the lawyer and the office manager, the controller concludes that the economic impact is contingent upon the ability of the company to sublease the vacant offices. It is clear that the costs incurred to make lease payments on the vacant offices represent a loss to the company, since no revenues are being generated from these vacant buildings. The controller feels that she can rely upon the office manager's ability to estimate the number of offices that will not be subleased. The controller restates the research problem as follows:

"Should a contingent loss be recognized currently on future rental commitments on vacant offices and, if so, what amount should be recognized?"

Review of the Literature. From the analysis and statement of the problem, the controller identifies the following keywords to be used in the literature search:

Losses	Contingent Loss
Loss Recognition	Leases
Commitments	Rent Expense

Using keywords to locate citations is akin to traveling through a maze, with the researcher encountering cross references that circle back to original starting points and keywords that prove to be dead ends. The literature search must be conducted carefully and systematically. Otherwise, the process can be frustrating and inefficient.

The *Index to Accounting and Auditing Technical Pronouncements* will be used to demonstrate a systematic approach to conducting the literature search.

Figure 7-2 diagrams one path that could be taken through the Index. The diagram aids the researcher in conducting and documenting an efficient literature search. The starting point of the search is the list of keywords identified from the statement of the problem. As these terms are reviewed for relevant citations, cross-references to other terms — broader, narrower, or related — are found in the Index. These additional terms are then examined for potential citations. The Index citations are listed alphabetically by authoritative source. The reader can determine the authoritative weight of each citation directly from the Index.

When the researcher feels that all relevant citations have been identified, the next step is to locate and review the authoritative literature. All the citations in Figure 7-2 reference sections of the *FASB Accounting Standards — Current Text*.

Section C59, "Contingencies," includes two relevant authoritative pronouncements — FASB Statement No. 5 and FASB Interpretation No. 14. The Topical Index of the *Current Text* can be used to locate specific paragraphs within this section. The paragraph references are located in the Topical Index under the keyword "Contingencies." It should be noted that the keywords used in topical indices do not necessarily correspond to those used in the *Index to Accounting and Auditing Technical Pronouncements*. A reference matrix similar to that shown in Figure 7-3 can be constructed to facilitate identification of section refer-

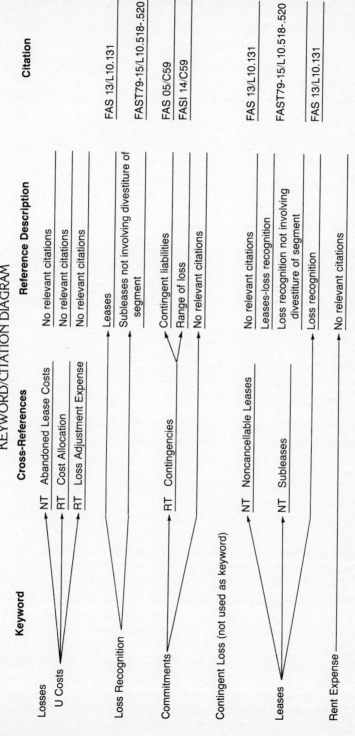

Figure 7-2

KEYWORD/CITATION DIAGRAM

Keyword	Cross-References	Reference Description	Citation
Losses			
U Costs	NT Abandoned Lease Costs	No relevant citations	
	RT Cost Allocation	No relevant citations	
	RT Loss Adjustment Expense	No relevant citations	
Loss Recognition		Leases	FAS 13/L10.131
		Subleases not involving divestiture of segment	FAST79-15/L10.518-.520
Commitments	RT Contingencies	Contingent liabilities	FAS 05/C59
		Range of loss	FASI 14/C59
		No relevant citations	
Contingent Loss (not used as keyword)			
Leases	NT Noncancellable Leases	No relevant citations	FAS 13/L10.131
	NT Subleases	Leases-loss recognition	
		Loss recognition not involving divestiture of segment	FAST79-15/L10.518-.520
		Loss recognition	
Rent Expense		No relevant citations	FAS 13/L10.131

Figure 7-3

REFERENCE MATRIX

	REFERENCE		
KEYWORD	Current Text Section	FASB Statement No. 5	FASB Interpretation No. 14
Contingencies			
Accrual of Loss Contingencies	C59.105-.107	Par. 8	Par. 2-3
	C59.109-.110	Par. 9-10	
	C59.124-.127		Par. 4-7
Definition	C59.101	Par. 1	
Estimation of Amount of Loss	C59.106-.107		Par. 2-3
	C59.124-.127		Par. 4-7
Probability of Future Events	C59.104	Par. 3	

ences and original pronouncements. Following is a summary of the relevant portions of the literature.

A loss contingency as defined in FASB Statement No. 5, paragraph 1, is an existing condition, situation, or set of circumstances involving uncertainty as to possible loss to an enterprise that will ultimately be resolved when one or more future events occur or fail to occur.

FASB Statement No. 5, paragraph 8, states that an estimated loss from a loss contingency should be accrued by a charge to income if both the following conditions are met:

1. It is *probable* that a loss has been incurred, i.e., future events confirming the loss are likely to occur.
2. The amount of loss can be reasonably estimated.

FASB Interpretation No. 14 clarifies the point that a loss should be accrued even if no single amount for the loss can be estimated. If only a range of potential loss can be estimated, the minimum amount should be accrued.

After reviewing relevant sections in the *Current Text*, the researcher could read the original pronouncements—FASB Statement No. 5 and Interpretation No. 14—to obtain additional insight into the background and rationale underlying the standards.

Survey of Present Practices. The researcher could review issues of *Accounting Trends & Techniques* for examples of reporting practices and disclosures for contingent liabilities. FASB Statement No. 5 and the interpretation of that standard require a disclosure of the nature of the contingent liability and the amount of loss that is possible above the amount of loss accrued in the financial statements.

Evaluation of Results. The initial concern was whether or not any loss should be recognized currently on the lease commitments on vacant offices. Through the examination of related documents and discussions with persons involved with the transactions the following facts were identified:

1. The realty company has an enforceable obligation to make the lease payments on the vacant offices.
2. The payments will represent a loss to the company because no revenues will be generated by the costs incurred.
3. The amount of the loss is contingent upon the ability of the realty company to sublease the offices. A reasonable estimate is that a maximum of 5 buildings could be subleased, and it is possible that none will be subleased.

The literature search has provided authoritative support for recognizing a contingent loss. The amount of the loss is to be measured by the minimum amount for the range of the estimated loss. There was no support in the literature for considering the rental payments as period costs to be recognized as expense when paid. Section L10.518-.520 was identified as a reference in Figure 7-2. Section L10.518-.520 is an FASB Technical Bulletin which is an unofficial interpretation of FASB Statement No. 13. The interpretation addresses the loss on a sublease not involved in a disposal of a business segment. It states that a loss should be recognized in a sublease to follow the general principle of providing for losses when it is reasonable to assume they have occurred. This same reasoning can be extended to the problem at hand where there will be no sublease payments to reduce the amount of the loss.

Conclusion and Documentation. The authoritative literature found through the research process supports accrual of the loss on the lease agreements. The amount of the loss should be the minimum of the range of the contingent loss. The financial statements should disclose the nature of the contingent loss and the amount of potential loss above the amount accrued in the financial statements. The following is a research memorandum that could be used for documenting the research process.

To: Alex Keller, President
From: Elaine Wise, Controller

At your request, I have researched the following matter to determine the impact on Keller Realty. The specific issue researched concerns whether a loss should be recognized currently on the rental commitments on the vacant offices. If recognition is required, what amount should be accrued?

In researching the authoritative literature, the following keywords were utilized: Losses, Loss Recognition, Commitments,

Contingent Loss, Leases, and Rent Expense. FASB Statement No. 5, "Accounting for Contingencies," states that a loss contingency should be accrued by a charge to income if (1) it is probable that a loss has been incurred and (2) the amount of the loss can be reasonably estimated. FASB Interpretation No. 14, "Reasonable Estimate of the Amount of Loss," states that a loss should be accrued even if no single amount for the loss can be estimated. If only a range of the potential loss can be estimated, the minimum amount should be accrued.

Keller Realty Inc. has an enforceable obligation to make the lease payments on the vacant offices, and no revenues will be generated by the costs incurred. It is reasonably estimated that from zero to 5 buildings could be subleased. The authoritative literature supports the accrual of a loss for the vacant lease offices. The amount of the loss will be the minimum estimate of the range of potential loss. Since the lease obligations extend over more than one accounting period, the accrual will be at the present value of the lease payments discounted at the Realty Company's marginal borrowing rate.

	Number of Leases	Monthly Rate	Months	P.V. Factor of Annuity Due at 1½%	P.V. Amount
Additional units:					
Subleased	5	$1500	3*	2.9560	$ 22,170
Not subleased	5	1500	60	39.9710	299,782
Not subleased	5	2500	60	39.9710	499,637
Loss accrual					$ 821,589
Potential additional loss	5	$1500	57	38.7059	290,294
					$1,111,883
Current portion	5	$1500	3	2.9560	$ 22,170
of loss	5	1500	12	11.0711	83,033
recognized	5	2500	12	11.0711	138,389
					$ 243,592

*Since 5 units are expected to be subleased within 6 months, the vacancy period on these units is averaged at 3 months.

The financial statement presentation and proper footnote disclosure should appear as follows:

Financial Statement Presentation and Disclosure

Income statement:
Revenues XXXX
Operating expenses:
    Loss on lease commitments $821,589

Balance sheet:
Current liabilities:
    Current portion of lease commitment.......... $243,592
    Long-term portion of lease commitments 577,997

<u>Notes</u>

Contingent Liabilities—The company has entered into certain lease agreements that have 5-year noncancellable terms remaining. Some of these offices are currently neither used nor subleased. The present value of the potential rental liability above the amount accrued is $290,294.

Keeping Current

In concluding this text, the authors would like to emphasize the importance of keeping current with the ever-expanding accounting and auditing pronouncements and to share with the reader some techniques which have been used successfully by various practitioners. Adopting one or a combination of the following techniques may save valuable time to spend possibly on the golf course rather than reading volume upon volume of materials attempting to stay current.

1. Checklists—Some practitioners develop a checklist for keeping current. A listing of new pronouncements is prepared and updated periodically with an indication as to which clients this pronouncement may affect. Pronouncements having no direct immediate impact on any client are placed in a "rainy day" reading file.

2. Pronouncement summaries—Some firms have developed in-house staff memos that are prepared by certain individuals periodically (e.g., weekly) and distributed to all staff members. Such memos identify new pronouncements and provide a brief summary write-up of each new pronouncement.

3. Reading of periodicals—Many business and accounting periodicals report summaries or the full text of new pronouncements. The practice of reading certain periodicals, such as the *Journal of Accountancy, Financial Executive,* and the *Wall Street Journal,* will aid the practitioner in the attempt to keep current.

Keeping up to date on the details of all new pronouncements is an impossibility. However, every practitioner must develop and consistently use a technique to keep as current as possible, especially with pronouncements that directly affect clients.

Summary

The accountant or auditor who attempts to keep current and has developed skills in researching accounting and auditing issues will be well rewarded by having obtained the confidence and respect of management and colleaques. Such respect is generally reserved for the truly professional accountant or auditor. This text attempts to aid the practitioner in fulfilling his or her professional role, which includes that of a competent researcher in accounting and auditing matters.

Appendix A

Case 1—Patrick Fabricating Company[1]

An audit client, Patrick Fabricating Company, has recently changed its method of valuing work-in-process inventories. Patrick had been using a percentage of direct labor in determining the amount of overhead to allocate to the work-in-process inventories. The percentage-of-direct labor method became unacceptable because the concept became too broad. As a result, Patrick Fabricating has refined the overhead allocation method in order to better calculate overhead for various types of jobs. Due to these refinements, overhead in work-in-process inventories has decreased.

As a result of the decrease in inventory valuation, Patrick's controller has requested advice as to whether this decrease is considered a change in accounting estimate or a correction of an error in previously issued financial statements. Furthermore, the controller requests an analysis of the impact, if any, that this inventory adjustment will have on the year's audit report.

Case 2—R. R. Watts Builders

R. R. Watts Builders purchased undeveloped land in Cooper, Tennessee last January. The land is included in Watts' current balance sheet at a value of $1,800,000 which represents its cost. Watts hired Thomas Battle, a qualified independent appraiser, to appraise the land, and Battle confirmed the $1,800,000 figure as accurate. However, this amount is contingent on securing zoning which will allow Watts to construct townhouses on the property. If the zoning is not obtained, the land will be worth no more than $1,000,000.

At a public hearing, the Cooper City Planning Commission recommended that the City Council, who has the final zoning authority, approve the proposed zoning. Upon request by the Council, the city's attorney has drafted an ordinance that would accomplish the rezoning. R. R. Watts Builders has received a letter from its attorney which states that the action by the Cooper City Council may not be binding due to

---

[1]These cases have been adapted from inquiries included in the AICPA's *Technical Practice Aids*.

possible court action. He also states that the chances of approval of the rezoning are good, but he cannot say what the city council's final decision will be.

As the auditor for R. R. Watts Builders, you are faced with the decision as to the type of audit report to issue. The land is a material item on Watts' balance sheet.

Appendix B

Solution to Case 1—Patrick Fabricating Company

Preliminary Problem Identification
How is a change in the allocation of overhead handled?

Problem Analysis
1. Due to the refinement of the method for allocating overhead to work in process, inventory costs have decreased.
2. The change may result in a modification of the auditor's report, if the change is considered a consistency qualification.

Refined Statement of the Problem
Is a change in the allocation of overhead to work in process considered to be a change in estimate, a change in accounting principle, or a correction of an error? What is the impact on the auditor's report?

Keywords
Following are some keywords that could be used in the literature search:

> Accounting Changes
> Error Correction
> Inventory Costing
> Consistency
> Inventories

Literature Search
A keyword/citation diagram (Figure 7-2) and a reference matrix (Figure 7-3) can be constructed to facilitate an orderly and efficient search for authoritative literature. The path followed in the literature search will vary according to the keywords selected and the indices used to locate citations.

Since the problem involves both accounting and auditing issues, the research will entail a review of literature in both the *AICPA Professional Standards* and the *FASB Accounting Standards—Current Text*. The AU Topical Index of the *Professional Standards* and the Topical Index of the *Current Text* could be used to locate citations. However, the *Index to Accounting and Auditing Technical Pronouncements* could be consulted first, since this publication is a comprehensive index of authoritative and semiauthoritative accounting and auditing pronouncements from a variety of sources.

Regardless of the initial keywords selected or the indices used, the literature search should lead the researcher to the following pronouncements:

1. APB Opinion No. 20—*Current Text* Section A06 (various paragraphs) and Section A35.104.
2. FASB Interpretation No. 1—*Current Text* Section A06.108.
3. Statement on Auditing Standards No. 1—*Professional Standards* AU Section 420.06.

Review of Literature

Relevant portions of the authoritative literature are discussed briefly in the following sections.

APB Opinion No. 20, "Accounting Changes"—Paragraph 6 of Opinion No. 20 (A06.104) defines an accounting change as a change in (1) an accounting principle, (2) an accounting estimate, or (3) a reporting entity. The correction of an error in previously issued financial statements is not considered an accounting change.

Paragraph 7 (A06.105) defines a change in accounting principle as a change resulting from the adoption of a generally accepted accounting principle different from the one used previously. The term "accounting principle" includes not only the principles and practices but also the methods of applying them.

Paragraph 13 of Opinion No. 20 (A35.104) identifies errors as those resulting from mathematical mistakes, mistakes in the application of accounting principles, or oversight or misuse of facts that existed at the time the financial statements were prepared.

FASB Interpretation No. 1, "Accounting Changes Related to the Cost of Inventory"—Paragraph 5 of Interpretation No. 1 (A06.108) states that a change in the composition of the elements of cost included in inventory is a change in accounting principle.

Statement on Auditing Standards No. 1—AU Section 420.06— Concerning the impact of an accounting change on the audit report, AU Section 420.06 states that a change in accounting principle, which includes the method of applying a principle, requires recognition in the auditor's report as to consistency.

Conclusion

The change in inventory cost allocation by Patrick Fabricating Company is a change in accounting principle and not a change in estimate or correction of an error. The change requires a qualification as to consistency in the auditor's report.

RESEARCH MEMORANDUM

Patrick Fabricating Company has requested our advice as to the proper treatment of a change in the allocation of overhead to work in process. The specific issue is whether this change is a change in estimate, a change in principle, or a correction of an error in previously issued financial statements. Also of concern is the impact the change may have on the current year's audit report.

In searching the literature, the following keywords were utilized: Accounting Changes, Error Correction, Inventory Costing, Consistency, and Inventories. FASB Interpretation No. 1, "Accounting Changes Related to the Cost of Inventory," specifically states that a change in the composition of the elements of cost included in inventory is an accounting change. Also, APB Opinion No. 20, "Accounting Changes," identifies Patrick's change as a change in the method of applying an accounting principle, which should be handled as a change in principle. Therefore, the change in the allocation of overhead is a change in accounting principle and not a change in estimate or a correction of an error.

As to the impact on the audit report, SAS No. 1, AU Section 420, states that a change in an accounting principle requires recognition as to consistency. Therefore, the audit report would be a qualified report.

Solution to Case 2 — R. R. Watts Builders

Preliminary Problem Identification

Can an unqualified audit opinion be issued on the financial statements of R. R. Watts?

Problem Analysis

1. Land may be significantly overvalued on the balance sheet.
2. If desired rezoning is not obtained, a write-off of $800,000 will be charged to income.

Refined Statement of the Problem

Land is currently carried on the balance sheet at its cost of $1,800,000. This amount equals the appraised value of the land, contingent upon rezoning which would permit construction of townhouses on the land. What is the effect, if any, on the audit report of the uncertainty regarding the valuation of the land?

Keywords

Following are some keywords that could be used in the literature search:

Audited Financial Statements
Audit Report
Contingencies
Uncertainties

Literature Search

A search of the *Index to Accounting and Auditing Technical Pronouncements* and/or the AU Topical Index of the *Professional Standards* should lead the researcher to Statement on Auditing Standards (SAS) No. 2, AU Section 509.

Review of Literature

AU Sections 509.21-.25 and .35 are applicable to the auditor's question. The following is a synopsis of these sections.

AU Section 509.21 — In preparing financial statements, management is expected to estimate the outcome of future events. Usually the auditor can obtain assurance that management's estimates are reasonable by considering audit evidence. Matters are not considered uncertainties unless management is not able to reasonably estimate the outcome. If the auditor disagrees with management's estimate and the financial statements are materially affected, the auditor should express an adverse or qualified opinion.

AU Section 509.22 — When management is not able to make a reasonable estimation as to the outcome of a matter that may materially affect the financial statements or required disclosures, the situation should be regarded as an uncertainty. When this uncertainty exists, a determination cannot be made as to whether financial statements should be adjusted or in what amount.

AU Section 509.23 — Specific uncertainties whose possible effects on the financial statements can be isolated can therefore be readily understood. There may also be uncertainties that are complex, making it difficult to determine the effects on the financial statements. If the uncertainties are material, their nature and possible effects should be disclosed in the financial statements.

AU Section 509.24 — An auditor, when forming an opinion, is not expected to predict the outcome of future events if management is not able to do so. When material uncertainties do exist, the auditor should decide upon an unqualified or qualified opinion. If he or she believes the outcome will not have a material affect on the financial statements, the auditor does not need to modify the opinion.

AU Section 509.25 — When considering uncertainties, the auditor should be able to determine whether the financial statement items affected have been stated in conformity with generally accepted accounting principles, except for those contingent upon the outcome of the uncertainty. If they do conform with generally accepted accounting principles, the auditor can express a qualified opinion based on an uncertainty. If the auditor does not believe that generally accepted accounting principles have been followed, the report should be modified accordingly.

AU Section 509.35 — When qualifying an opinion, the auditor should use the phrase "except for" unless the qualification is the result of an uncertainty. In this case, the expression "subject to" should be used.

Evaluation and Conclusion

AU Sections 509.21, .22, .24, and .35 on uncertainties provide answers to the question. Considering these citations, three important aspects to this problem are: (1) Does management feel confident and have enough information as to the outcome? (2) Are all other financial statement items stated in conformity with generally accepted accounting principles? (3) Is the amount material?

First, as stated in paragraphs .21 and .22, if the client is reasonably sure of the estimation and the auditor agrees, an unqualified opinion can be issued. If the client cannot be reasonably sure of the outcome of the event, then a qualified opinion must be given. Secondly, the auditor should determine whether all other financial statement items are stated in accordance with generally accepted accounting principles. If so, he or she can express a qualified opinion based on the uncertainty. Finally, materiality is important because it is also a determining factor in the opinion given. The following is stated in paragraph .24, "The auditor need not modify his opinion because of the existence of an uncertainty when he concludes that there is minimal likelihood that resolution of the uncertainty will have a material effect on the financial statements." Therefore, if the event is not material, the auditor may issue an unqualified opinion regardless of the uncertainty. However, if it has been determined that an uncertainty exists and the amount is material, a qualified opinion should be expressed.

Paragraph .35 specified how a qualified opinion should be worded. In the case of an uncertainty, "subject to" is the appropriate wording for the qualification.

In the situation of R. R. Watts Builders, it would probably be concluded that there is significant uncertainty as to securing the proper zoning. There is no mention of any other problems with the affected financial statements besides the contingency. Therefore, it can be assumed that the other items are in conformance with generally accepted accounting principles. From the above conclusions, the auditor should express a qualified, "subject to" opinion on the financial statements.

RESEARCH MEMORANDUM

R. R. Watts Builders has valued the purchase of undeveloped land at $1.8 million. However, the land's value will be only $1 million if a favorable zoning change is not approved by the Cooper City Council. Research was conducted to determine what effect, if any, the uncertainty regarding the land valuation would have on the type of audit report issued.

The $800,000 difference in the value of the undeveloped land if the zoning change is not approved, is a material amount to Watts. All

other financial statement items are recorded in accordance with
generally accepted accounting principles. Watts cannot reasonably
estimate the outcome of the zoning issue. Additionally, their attorney states that the action of the City Council may not be binding due
to possible court action.

Based on a review of SAS No. 2 (AU Sections 509.21-.25, .35),
the facts presented in the Watts audit should be considered as an
uncertainty. Thus, according to our research, we should issue a
qualified, "subject to" opinion and request that adequate disclosure of
this item be reported in a footnote to the financial statements.

DATE DUE

MAY 1 5 1991			
	45230		Printed in USA